TAKE-HOME CHEMISTRY:

50

Low-Cost Activities to Extend Classroom Learning

TAKE-HOME CHEMISTRY:

50 Low-Cost Activities to Extend Classroom Learning

NSTA press

National Science Teachers Association

Arlington, Virginia

Michael Horton

Claire Reinburg, Director
Jennifer Horak, Managing Editor
Andrew Cooke, Senior Editor
Wendy Rubin, Associate Editor
Agnes Bannigan, Associate Editor
Amy America, Book Acquisitions Coordinator

ART AND DESIGN
Will Thomas Jr., Director
Illustrations by Linda Olliver

SCILINKS
Tyson Brown, Director
Virginie L. Chokouanga, Customer Service and Database Coordinator

PRINTING AND PRODUCTION
Catherine Lorrain, Director
Jack Parker, Electronic Prepress Technician

NATIONAL SCIENCE TEACHERS ASSOCIATION
Francis Q. Eberle, PhD, Executive Director
David Beacom, Publisher
1840 Wilson Blvd., Arlington, VA 22201
www.nsta.org/store
For customer service inquiries, please call 800-277-5300.

Library of Congress Cataloging-in-Publication Data
Horton, Michael, 1972-
  Take-home chemistry : 50 low-cost activities to extend classroom learning / by Michael Horton.
    p. cm.
  Includes bibliographical references and index.
  ISBN 978-1-936137-39-8
  1. Chemistry--Experiments--Laboratory manuals. 2. Chemistry--Study and teaching (Secondary)--Activity programs. I. Title.
  QD43.H67 2011
  540.7--dc23
                    2011034480

eISBN 978-1-936959-94-5

NSTA is committed to publishing material that promotes the best in inquiry-based science education. However, conditions of actual use may vary, and the safety procedures and practices described in this book are intended to serve only as a guide. Additional precautionary measures may be required. NSTA and the authors do not warrant or represent that the procedures and practices in this book meet any safety code or standard of federal, state, or local regulations. NSTA and the authors disclaim any liability for personal injury or damage to property arising out of or relating to the use of this book, including any of the recommendations, instructions, or materials contained therein.

 Featuring SciLinks—a new way of connecting text and the Internet. Up-to-the minute online content, classroom ideas, and other materials are just a click away. For more information, go to www.scilinks.org/Faq.aspx.

TABLE OF CONTENTS

INTRODUCTION

SECTION 1: Science Process Skills, Measurement, and Scientific Inquiry

SECTION 2: Chemical and Physical Properties

SECTION 3: Chemical Reactions

SECTION 4: Gas Laws, pH, and Kinetic Molecular Theory

INTRODUCTION

Research has shown that homework can be an effective and meaningful learning tool for high school students if it is relevant, engaging, and hands-on. These take-home chemistry activities are designed to match those criteria. The activities also cost far less than $10 per student the first year, and only a small amount each year after to refill the consumables. Educational writer Alfie Kohn said in a 2006 interview that there are only two ways that homework is effective for high school students. One way is using "activities that have to be done at home, such as … a science experiment in the kitchen" (Oleck 2006). This book is a collection of such activities.

This book is a collection of chemistry labs that lend themselves to being performed at home with simple materials. It is not intended to be a chemistry textbook or to cover every topic encountered in high school chemistry. Most of the labs are written as structured or Level 2 inquiry (see Inquiry in Chemistry, page xiii), and some include instructions to raise the level of inquiry if the teacher feels comfortable doing so. A few activities just are not compatible with inquiry at home and are written as Level 1 labs but are still important because they introduce topics critical for other experiments or topics that have common misconceptions. Most of the activities involve measuring, graphing, calculating, extrapolating graphs, and performing other science-process skills.

Because this is one piece of a complete chemistry curriculum, it is assumed that traditional learning and hands-on activities in the classroom will fill in where take-home labs are not practical. Teachers may choose to eliminate some of the labs and substitute others without breaking the flow of the labs. Used in this way, the hands-on activities can be a powerful tool for learning chemistry concepts and preparing students for chemistry standardized assessments that are highly dependent on charts, graphs, and conceptual questions. These activities have been piloted in schools across the United States and used by teachers who received the material during conference presentations. The success that these teachers have had with the labs helps refute the common misconception among teachers and students that lectures are for learning and labs are for fun. Students *can* learn chemistry from labs.

Although the labs are written as take-home activities for high school students, many of the activities in the book are well suited for homeschooled students as well as those who take online courses. These activities would also be appropriate for family science nights and museum outreach programs. If a teacher does not have sufficient materials to send an activity home with every student, the lab could be performed in class as an alternative. One teacher used the activities in after-school intervention programs for students who were not proficient after being exposed to the concepts in the classroom.

Why Take-Home Labs?

These take-home labs, if implemented effectively, can address most or all of the following problems, which are common with chemistry labs and homework.

Students will not do homework. This sentiment could be rephrased as *Students will not do busy work at home*. When presented with fun and challenging assignments that open doors to understanding the physical world around them, students will rise to the occasion. Throughout four years of implementing these activities, I found that the homework completion rate improved greatly, and test scores indicate that student achievement increased as well (see Evidence of Success below).

Students do poorly on standardized tests. Most standardized science tests are weighted toward science-process skills. These skills include drawing and interpreting charts and graphs, finding patterns, interpreting diagrams, and analyzing experimental data. The take-home labs in this book support each of these skills.

There is not enough class time to cover all the standards. A great deal of class time is used on simple labs that students could do at home. These labs are important, but they consume valuable class time. By having students perform these labs at home, teachers recover days of class time in which new concepts can be taught or reinforced.

Students do not experience enough labs. By assigning take-home lab work, teachers can increase the number of labs students complete over the course of the year. This will lead to a more engaging, fulfilling learning experience for students, which will lead to deeper, longer-lasting learning.

Chemistry labs are expensive. There are 50 labs in this book, and the collection of materials needed to complete the labs costs $10 or less, or approximately 20¢ per lab per student the first year. After the first year, only breakages and consumables need to be replaced, at a cost of less than a dollar per kit.

Chemistry students lack basic skills when they get to my class. Some of the take-home labs teach about background information and skills that students are supposed to remember from middle school but rarely do. These labs are a good refresher that you can refer back to throughout the year. As mentioned earlier, it can also buy you extra days of class time to teach the chemistry curriculum for your grade level.

My school will not let me do take-home labs because of No Child Left Behind. NCLB prohibits some schools from allowing take-home labs because the materials are not provided to every student. That practice, it is argued, puts some students at a disadvantage. However, teachers can easily provide almost every object needed to do *Take-Home Chemistry* labs, with the exception of a couple of labs that require students to provide water or other common materials. If students inform the teacher in advance that they do not have certain required items at home, the teacher can provide these materials as well. Appropriate safety precautions should be followed if and when the teacher sends household chemicals home with students.

Evidence of Success

A chemistry teaching colleague and I have informally collected data on the success of these take-home labs. We began by sending individual activities home in sandwich bags in 2003 and increased the number and quality of the activities over the next several years. Most chemistry students were 10th and 11th graders. As shown in Figure 1.1, four years of implementing chemistry take-home labs coincided with a more than tenfold increase from 3% to 32% (solid box) in the proportion of proficient and advanced students in chemistry based on the 2002 baseline. In the same time period, the number of students testing below basic and far below basic decreased dramatically from 53% to 17% (dashed box).

Figure 1.1

Chemistry Proficiency Before, During, and After Implementation

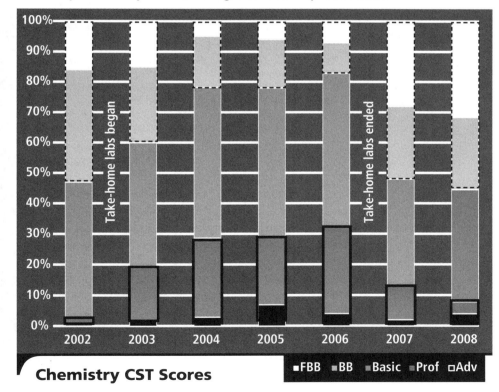

FBB = Far Below Basic, BB = Below Basic, Prof = Proficient, and Adv = Advanced. California considers FBB, BB, and Basic to be nonproficient.

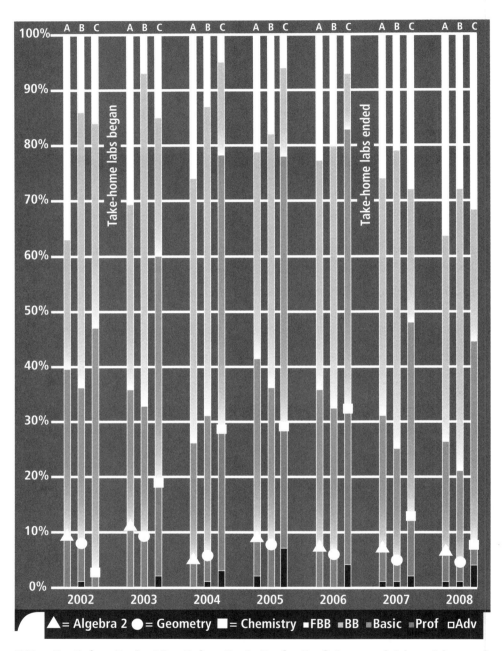

Figure 1.2

Comparison of Student Proficiency in Chemistry, Geometry, and Algebra 2

▲ = Algebra 2 ● = Geometry ■ = Chemistry ■FBB ■BB ■Basic ■Prof □Adv

FBB = Far Below Basic, BB = Below Basic, Prof = Proficient, and Adv = Advanced. California considers FBB, BB, and Basic to be nonproficient.

To strengthen the argument that the score changes were due to the take-home labs and not to other changes in the school or the student body, student performance in Algebra 2 and Geometry over the same period was examined (see Figure 1.2). Those scores stayed nearly the same over this time period. Most chemistry students are in either Algebra 2 or Geometry.

Although I left the classroom early in the 2005–2006 school year, my chemistry colleague collaborated with the long-term substitute teacher and continued the take-home labs. Figure 1.1 shows that in 2007, when the chemistry colleague became an administrator and the take-home labs ended, the test scores went back to almost where they had been before we started. That trend continued in 2008.

During implementation of these activities, this high school was a state-identified underperforming school with more than 70% of the students qualifying for free or reduced-price lunch. More than 40% of parents never graduated from high school and more than 25% of students are English language learners. The state also puts schools into groups of 100 similar schools based on dozens of criteria. My school had far higher chemistry scores than those similar schools, as much as a 156-times-larger ratio of proficient and advanced students to below-basic and far-below-basic students. Overall, the school was ranked in the second decile from the bottom in the state in 2006. In chemistry, the school was above the state average, putting it at least five deciles from the bottom.

In short, the chemistry scores at this school were above school, district, county, and state averages despite lower scores in other subjects schoolwide. Although the same results cannot be guaranteed at every site, this program was highly effective for these teachers and these groups of diverse students.

All data in Figures 1.1 and 1.2 were taken from the California Department of Education website (*cde.ca.gov*) for Perris High School in the Perris Union High School District in Riverside County, California.

Inquiry in Chemistry

The topic of inquiry in science instruction—what it looks like, how best to implement it in the classroom, ways to assess its success—far exceeds the scope of this introduction. The following is a brief explanation of inquiry and how I define it in this volume. For a full and more detailed discussion of inquiry, please consult the resources list.

When inquiry is discussed in science education, it has two meanings. The first meaning is the creation of an atmosphere of inquiry in the classroom in which students interact with one another and the teacher facilitates open-ended investigation of student-generated questions daily. The second use of the term refers to inquiry activities. This book alone cannot accomplish the first task, but it is intended to provide the second. The post-lab questions take the place of the teacher's guiding questions during an inquiry activity performed in the classroom. Although both forms of inquiry are valuable and effective, this book only aims to provide structured inquiry activities to be used as high-level, hands-on homework and practice.

It is a common misconception that inquiry is all or nothing. Most of the research about inquiry activities identifies four levels of inquiry (Banchi and Bell 2008; Colburn 2000; McComas 2005), although the first level is not inquiry at all (see Figure 1.3). What changes at each level is how much information is given to the student (i.e., the question, the procedure, the answer) (Bell, Smetana, and Binns 2005). Herron (1971) first described inquiry by distinguishing among three different levels. Since then, rubrics and matrices have been created with three, four, five, and seven levels (Lee et al. 2001). Because most education researchers refer to four levels, that is the model that will be used in this book.

Figure 1.3

What Is Provided to Students at the Different Levels of Inquiry

	Question Given	Procedure Given	Answer Known
Level 1	X	X	X
Level 2	X	X	
Level 3	X		
Level 4			

Level 1 inquiry activities are also known as verification, or "cookbook," activities. In a Level 1 activity, students are given the question or problem and the procedure, and they already know the answer to the question. They simply verify something they have already learned. Technically, the activities are not inquiry at all. This is not to say that they are completely ineffective, but not as effective as higher levels of inquiry.

In a **Level 2**, or "structured inquiry," activity, students are given the question and procedure, but they do not yet know the answer. Having students perform an activity before learning the concept raises the activity to Level 2. In performing this significant step, the teacher is giving all students the same background knowledge, an activity on which to hang the concept in their memory, and a common experience to refer back to in class when covering or practicing the concept. Robert Marzano (2004, p. 3) says, "Students who have a great deal of background knowledge in a given subject area are likely to learn new information readily and quite well. The converse is also true." Dochy, Segers, and Buehl (1999) found through meta-analysis that differences in students' prior knowledge explain 81% of the variance in post-test scores. The research of Langer (1984) and Stevens (1980) shows a well-established correlation between prior knowledge and academic achievement.

Most of the labs in this book are written as Level 2 inquiry, which means the teacher must assign the activities to students before teaching the concept in class. Assigning the activities this way increases the level of inquiry and also allows teachers to afford students prior knowledge when the concept is covered formally in class later. Marzano states that "what students *already know* about the content is one of the strongest indicators of how well they will learn new information relative to the content" (2004, p. 1). Douglas Llewellyn, in *Teaching High School Science Through Inquiry: A Case Study Approach* (2005), recommends doing the lab first to raise the inquiry level. Bell (Bell, Smetana, and Binns 2005, p. 33) comments, "The difference between a Level 1 and Level 2 activity can be a matter of timing. A confirmation lab can become a structured inquiry lab by simply presenting the lab before the target concept is taught." To get the full effect from these activities, teachers are expected to use them in this way. Teachers who are uncomfortable with this method are welcome to use them as cookbook labs, but should not expect the same results.

As Level 2 inquiry activities, deep explanations are not included, as that would lower them to Level 1. As such, it is expected that the teacher will use these activities as introductions to topics and give formal instruction after the activity to take advantage of the prior knowledge gained.

In a **Level 3** activity, referred to as "guided inquiry," students are given an appropriate question and asked to determine the procedure and develop the answer on their own. Many activities in this book can be converted to Level 3 simply by removing the procedure and having students determine how to accomplish the task. For example, a lab inviting students to follow a procedure to determine what affects the rate of a chemical reaction could be increased to Level 3 by changing the activity to "Which affect(s) the rate of a chemical reaction—particle size, temperature, or stirring?" and having students determine an appropriate procedure. Some of these take-home labs are already Level 3, and teachers are free to modify others to meet the Level 3 criteria. Most of the extension activities, which are often provided at the end of the activities, are opportunities for Level 3 inquiry, and several of the post-lab questions encourage students to test ideas on their own. Teachers can remove some steps in the procedure, add unnecessary steps and have students identify them, remove data tables and have students create their own, add extensions, or rearrange the steps to transition to Level 3 gradually (Llewellyn 2005). Some of the labs in this book already require students to create their own data charts.

In a **Level 4** activity, referred to as "open inquiry," students pose their own question and are given the resources to answer that question. This type of inquiry is most easily demonstrated with science fair projects. Students investigate their own questions by following their own procedures and then draw their own conclusions.

Many teachers also use this type of inquiry as differentiated instruction activities. If a student clearly understands a concept while doing an inquiry lab, he or she may be invited to come up with additional questions to answer independently. It is not the intent of this book to provide Level 4 inquiry activities, but teachers are encouraged to motivate students to perform deeper follow-up activities to answer questions they may have after an activity. Students can certainly extend experiments to answer their own questions, hence independently creating their own Level 4 inquiry activities. Some of the extension activities could be replaced with a more general Level 4 question, such as "What other questions do you have about this topic? Create an activity that will lead you to the answer."

Some teachers are discouraged when they begin using inquiry activities and do not immediately see the achievement gains they expected. Students need experience using inquiry activities to learn. They do not relate classroom lab activities with learning because they have always done verification labs. I have seen low performance the first few times questions were given on a test about a subject learned via inquiry. However, when students were reminded of the activity, they immediately began writing again and performance increased greatly. After a little experience, students no longer need to be reminded and make the connection automatically.

Please be warned that providing question stems such as "Remembering the string and protractor lab …" is not intended to be a long-term strategy because high-stakes tests will not do so. Some of the labs in this book are Level 1. They are included to overcome student misconceptions, provide experiences that allow students to see chemistry phenomena, or enable students to collect and analyze data that will assist them in understanding a concept more thoroughly. Some topics just do not lend themselves well to inquiry at home, but they are far fewer than those topics that do.

Providing Feedback to Students

Keep in mind that feedback of some type should be given on each lab that students do. This can be time consuming but very valuable. The purpose of these labs is not to add more items to the teacher's grade book.

Homework should be used as formative assessment. Often, formative assessments are not even graded. The teacher uses them to judge where the students are in relation to proficiency on the relevant standard. If the purpose of the lab is to give common background information to the students, then the teacher may also consider this a situation that need not be graded formally at all. But keep in mind that whether the teacher grades the labs or not, there must be feedback in the classroom. Some teachers may choose to give the labs credit/no credit or credit/redo marks.

Marzano (2006) reports that students who do not receive feedback after a formative assessment do no better on the summative assessment than if they had not been given the formative assessment at all. He lists several different ways to offer that feedback and gives the pre- and post-test gains that can be expected. Just putting a grade at the top of the paper has a negative effect on summative test results. If the teacher decides to formally grade the labs, then the feedback should be deeper than a simple overall grade. Having students prepare short written summaries, explain their logic aloud to the class, or discuss the activities while the teacher rotates around the room to deal with misconceptions are examples of ways teachers can check for understanding without formal grading. It is also helpful for the teacher to identify the criteria used to deem a conclusion satisfactory and allow students to redo the activity until it is satisfactory. It is also beneficial to show students good and bad examples of lab reports. This simple practice will likely increase the percentage of good lab reports you will get.

Some schools have not gotten to the point where formative assessments are used this way, however. Teachers may want to give credit for these labs simply to encourage students to perform the labs. Although it is worth repeating that these activities do not have to be graded, following are some tips for easing that burden if the teacher chooses to do so. A compromise could be that the teacher only grades some of the labs but the students do not know in advance which labs will be graded.

Teachers should create a grading guide that identifies which parts of each lab are the most important and assesses only those parts. For those labs that are graded, not every section has to be graded. And for every section that is graded, not every question or detail has to be analyzed.

A grading guide could look something like this:

Name_____ Period_____

Building Your Balance
Data _____/ 5 Post-Lab Questions _____/5   **Total ____/10**

Thickness of Paper Lab
Data _____/5 Calculations _____/5   **Total ____/10**

Graphing the Ball's Bounce
Post-Lab Questions ____/5 Graphs ____/5   **Total ____/10**

Investigating an Urban Legend
Data ____/5 Conclusion ____/2   **Total ____/7**

The Mole
Data ____/2 Post-Lab Questions ____/5   **Total ____/7**

Calculating Moles Lab
not graded

Completeness and Setup of Lab Notebook   **Total ____/15**
                                                    Grand Total ____/59

Lab Notebooks

Because students may perform as many as 50 activities at home, a lab notebook is a useful tool for students to keep track of their lab write-ups. They are also great modeling for college and of how real science researchers work. Teachers may choose to collect the notebooks after, for example, 5 or 10 activities have been completed as a means of assessment. Feedback should be given after each activity; the teacher should not wait for five activities to be completed. The teacher should determine in advance the format for the notebooks (e.g., Purpose, Procedure, Data, Calculations, Safety Practices) and establish a set of rules for using the notebooks.

Figure 1.4

Small Sample of Materials for Lab Boxes

Figure 1.5

Some Items Ready to Distribute

These rules help students stay organized and save teachers time when reviewing the notebooks. The students' write-ups should include data charts, graphs, and post-lab questions as called for in a given activity's directions. Composition-style notebooks, spiral notebooks, or three-ring binders are all acceptable notebooks. Teachers may also consult their local university instructor to find out how freshmen are required to organize their notebooks, then ask their own students to set up their notebooks in a similar fashion.

Teachers are free to decide on their own whether the activities will be accomplished individually or in groups. If the teacher chooses for them to be completed individually, it is clear when students cheat on a take-home lab. For most of the labs, there is a small chance that any two people would get the exact same answer. If two students do get the exact same answers, it is clear they copied.

Again, it is not imperative to grade every lab or every part of those that are graded. Formal summative assessments will determine which students understood the concepts and which students did not. These labs are not about assigning grades. They are about learning chemistry. Each lab should be reviewed by the teacher to check for understanding, and feedback should be given in one form or another.

Tips for Using This Book

Teachers may opt to use *Take-Home Chemistry* labs exactly as they are presented or adapt them to better suit the needs of a particular class. Labs may be written on the board or posted via overhead projector for students to copy into their lab notebooks, or teachers may choose to pass out copies to each student. Teachers should let students know that any pages they need to write on or cut out will be given to them separately (those pages are included at the end of this book). Copies can be stored in materials boxes and reused from year to year.

Note: On the teacher pages, the objective will describe what the student is trying to accomplish and the purpose will describe the skill or concept they will learn. For example, sometimes the student will think the objective is to calculate the root mean path of atoms, but the purpose of the activity is for them to practice measuring in metric units and calculating averages.

Based on feedback I received about *Take-Home Physics,* the layout of this book has been changed so it is easier for teachers to use. Student activities are grouped together to ease the process of creating a student lab manual. The white space on the page is arranged so that no information is near the book's binding (allowing for easier photocopying). I hope these changes make this book convenient for the teacher to use. As mentioned above, pages that students will cut out or write on have been included at the back of the book for teachers to give students separately from the lab manual. You can photocopy page xxix to include at the beginning of the student manual

Assembling the Materials

Once you decide to assign the labs in this book, you will need to start planning. A list of materials is included on the teacher and student pages for each lab to assist teachers in determining what materials will be needed. A master materials list is included at the end of this section.

The basic idea is that you will send a (plastic, shoe-box size) box of materials home with the students that will enable them to complete all the activities in this book. The box is pictured in Figures 1.4 and 1.5 (p. xviii). Sending all the materials home in one box is preferable to sending individual activities home in plastic sandwich bags because of the time that it will take to check each bag in and out. If individual labs are all you can manage the first year, it is acceptable, but it will bring challenges to the situation (such as getting the materials returned to you). All the materials can fit into one box, which may be purchased for around a dollar, or, alternatively, a 1 gal. plastic freezer bag may be used.

After determining which labs you will assign and how much of each item is necessary, it's time to go shopping. Most of the items can be found at discount or 99-cent stores—from the boxes themselves to the batteries, salt, sugar, balloons, and Epsom salts. A couple of items, such as washers and nails, can be purchased at a home improvement store. Many items can be purchased at a much lower cost online than in stores or catalogs. For example, rubber balls can be purchased online inexpensively, but beware of high shipping costs. The website *www.rebeccas.com* sells 250 bouncy balls for around $22, including shipping. That's less than 9¢ each.

Be sure to buy a few extra of each item in case of loss and breakage. Once purchased, the items will take up quite a bit of space. (Figure 1.4 shows a small sample of the materials used to make lab boxes.) Do not plan to store them in the back of your classroom. (Tip: Purchase a few extra boxes to store items in while you dispense them.) Syringes are far less expensive on veterinary websites than from science suppliers.

When all materials have been purchased, put each item in its own box for easier distribution (see Figure 1.5). Find a large space to spread out the boxes in an assembly line so students can walk by, pick up the boxes, and fill them with the materials. Attach a 3 × 5 in. index card to each box with the quantity that students need to take written on it and instruct students to follow the cards in order (e.g., pick up six marbles, four paper clips, one rubber ball, etc.).

Remind students that they are to return all nonconsumable items with the boxes at the end of the year or upon transferring to another class or school. If not, they will be charged a fine such as for a lost or damaged textbook.

Master Materials List

Anything with a * next to it will be used up during the year. Anything with a + next to it will be returned at the end of the year.

Material	Source
+ Ruler (plastic with hole in center)	99¢ or discount store
* Small bathroom cups (4–6 if paper, 3 if plastic [like salsa containers])	Warehouse store
+ 60 ml syringe	Veterinary supply
+ Dental floss	99¢ store
+ 6 washers	Home improvement store
+ Rubber ball	Online
* Salt packet	Donated or warehouse store
* Sugar packet	Donated or warehouse store
* Zip-top bag with sand, salt, Styrofoam, iron	(see p. 45)
+ 6 marbles	99¢ store
* Coffee filter	99¢ store
* Transparent drinking straw	99¢ store
* 2 Wint-O-Green Life Savers	99¢ store
* Sugar cubes	Warehouse or grocery store
+Large plastic cup	99¢ store
*Effervescent tablet	99¢ store
*2 water balloons	99¢ store
*1 large balloon	99¢ store
*Zip-top bag with Epsom salts	99¢ store
*Zip-top bag with steel wool (must be real steel wool)	
+9 V battery	99¢ store
+Battery clip	Online or Radio Shack
+2 pieces of graphite (0.7 mm pencil lead)	99¢ store
*2 iron nails (shiny)	Home improvement store
*2 anodized nails (dull gray)	Home improvement store
+Mustard packet	Donated or warehouse store
*Minimarshmallow (provided later)	Grocery store
*pH paper (provided later)	Made by teacher (see p. 199)
*2 empty zip-top bags	99¢ store
+Syringe cap	Flinn Scientific
+Paper clip	99¢ store
*Waxed paper square	99¢ store
+Indirectly vented chemical splash goggles that meet ANSI Z87.1 standard	

Inexpensive sources for goggles include Gallaway Safety and Supply ($2.39, item #2235R); *www.envirosafetyproducts.com* ($1.94, SKU: PYRG204), and other similar websites.

Students will be expected to have the following items at home. If they do not, the teacher should have some extras to loan out.

- Vinegar
- Baking soda
- Ammonia
- Sugar
- Salt
- Cups or drinking glasses
- Coins
- Magnet
- Ink pens
- Scissors
- Ice cube
- Cooking oil
- Dishwashing liquid
- 2 L soda bottle
- Toaster or hair dryer
- Compact disk
- Shoe box
- Rubbing alcohol
- Fruit juice or colored drink (e.g., Gatorade)
- Soda
- Tape
- Cornstarch
- 100 pieces of rice, dried beans, popcorn kernels, or similar small objects
- Comb
- Thread
- Paper towels
- 3 × 5 in. card

Managing the Boxes

Before assigning take-home labs, consider how you will manage the boxes—especially how they will be collected at the end of the school year. Incomplete or lost boxes are a waste of time and money.

Make the distribution of box lids a routine part of the new school year. For example, if the school librarian manages textbook distribution and collection at your school, have that person also assist with the check-in and check-out process for your materials boxes. In my school, when students enrolled in chemistry and picked up their textbooks from the library, they also signed out the chemistry lab materials in the form of a box lid. That is, the lids were labeled with bar codes and checked out to students, and the boxes (in my classroom) were labeled with a matching bar code. When a student brought a lid to class, I gave him or her the matching box to be filled with materials. (Tip: Do not put the materials away yet, as you will certainly have students checking into your class late. Just put the lids on the boxes of extra materials and store them somewhere convenient.)

Even with such a system in place, you will need to keep careful watch over the boxes. Students may transfer out of the class or the school and take the box with them. If so, send a letter to their new classes (if they are still enrolled in the school), home, or new school asking for the boxes to be returned. If the boxes are still not returned, treat them just like a textbook and charge a fee to cover the loss. Students should not receive transfer grades until all debts are cleared, including the boxes. It is always preferable—and less costly—to get the box back rather than receive money for a new box.

Tell students at the beginning of the year that the boxes must be returned at the end of the year and some items will be used up while others will remain. Also tell them approximately how much each item is worth in case they are lost or broken. The librarian, or whoever collects textbooks at the end of the year, can charge these partial damages just like damage to a book. After students return the boxes, the teacher determines if all the materials are there and takes the lids and a list of missing items back to the library.

Do not wait until the last day of the school year to collect the boxes, as students inevitably will be absent or forget to bring their boxes. Rather, start collecting the boxes as soon as the last lab is finished. This will give you several weeks to collect them. Then students can drop off the individual materials in the summer storage boxes to be counted and refilled if necessary.

Safety Notes

Goggles

There are generally two philosophies on goggles. One is that students should wear goggles with all chemistry experiments, no matter what. The other is that students should be taught when goggles are necessary and when they are not. The author feels that the latter approach is far more responsible and teaches students lifelong lessons. However, if the former is the policy in your class, then feel free to require goggles on all experiments.

When purchasing goggles, the teacher should know that there is a big difference between impact goggles that keep objects from hitting the eye and chemical splash goggles that keep chemicals out of the eye. Chemical splash goggles are what

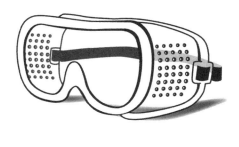

students need for these activities. The goggles should be indirectly vented and meet ANSI Z87.1 standard. The materials list gives sources of these goggles for less than $2 each.

Other Safety Notes

- If a student happens to get splashed with a hazardous material such as vinegar or ammonia, flush eyes directly with warm (60–100°F) tap water for a minimum of 15 minutes. Consult an emergency care provider if the eyes show symptoms such as burning or blurriness.
- There are possible choking hazards for very small children in the home. Emphasize to your students that the boxes of lab materials must be kept out of the reach of small children.
- Material Data Safety Sheets (MSDS) must be provided in kits as hard copy or online for any hazardous materials used, such as ammonia, rubbing alcohol, and vinegar. The teacher should review safety rules with students prior to performing the activity.
- Remind students not to drink or eat materials used in the lab. (The Wint-O-Green Life Savers are individually wrapped and should be sent home separately from the box so as not to send mixed messages.)
- At the end of each lab, students should be reminded to wash hands with soap and water.
- At the end of each lab, students need to appropriately discard all materials used.
- Immediately wipe up any liquid spilled on the floor to prevent slip-and-fall hazards.
- Remind students to use caution when working with sharp objects such as scissors, electrical wires, glass, and metal cans. These items may cut or puncture skin.
- On page xxviii is a label that should be on the top of all boxes before they are distributed. Just print the page onto peel-and-stick paper, cut out the stickers, and place a sticker on each box or lid. If the peel-and-stick paper is made for the computer printer, you may need to scan the page first.
- See page xxv for an acknowledgment form to parents that explains the possible dangers of the box of lab materials. It also notes the need for adult supervision on some activities. This letter should be sent home, signed by a parent or guardian, and returned by all students.

Dear Parent or Guardian:

Soon your child will bring home a box of materials to perform chemistry labs at home. These activities will give your child more skill in performing labs, analyzing data, and creating charts and graphs, and they will free up time in class to cover other important topics.

Although safety precautions and training have been provided by the teacher for all of the labs in an effort to help make them safer, there is always a chance that an accident can happen. Please encourage your child to use goggles when appropriate. There are some common household materials, such as ammonia and alcohol, that can be hazardous when used incorrectly. There also are small objects that could present a choking hazard for small children (such as marbles and a rubber ball).

The box will have a warning sticker on top to discourage young children from opening it. Students should keep the lid on the box at all times and keep the box out of the reach of children. Activities should be done under the supervision of an adult.

Sincerely,

I have read and understand and acknowledge that labs must be performed using appropriate safety equipment and following safety procedures, and under adult supervision. Abuse of laboratory instructions and/or safety training could possibly lead to harm. I do not hold the teacher, school, author, or publisher responsible for injuries sustained while performing these labs.

_____

Printed Name Parent   Student

_____

Signature   Date

Acknowledgments

Most of the ideas in this book have some basis in my experience as a teacher and teacher educator. I appreciate the contributions of other science authors, and it is my intent to try to provide credit where credit is due for the ideas. But many of these activities were in my lesson repertoire for many years, and the original source cannot be traced. The books and websites that are listed below are valuable resources, and the ideas for many of the labs may have originated in them.

Gardner, R. 1982. *Kitchen chemistry: Science experiments to do at home.* New York: Julian Messner.

Liem, T. 1987. *Invitations to science inquiry.* Lexington, MA: Ginn Press. *www. eric.ed.gov/ERICDocs/data/ericdocs2sql/content_storage_01/0000019b/80/1e/ 27/27.pdf.*

McMillan, M. 1992. *A demonstration a day ... for high school chemistry.* Battle Creek, MI: Calhoun Scientific.

Robinson, P. 2002. *Conceptual physics laboratory manual.* Needham, MA: Prentice Hall.

Towse, P. 1997. *A proceedings on cost-effective chemistry: Ideas for hands-on activities.* Madison, WI: Institute for Chemical Education.

United Nations Educational, Scientific and Cultural Organization (UNESCO). 1962. *700 science experiments for everyone.* Garden City, NY: Doubleday.

Wink et. al. 2005. *Working with chemistry: A laboratory inquiry program.* New York: W. H. Freeman and Company.

References

Banchi, H., and R. Bell. 2008. The many levels of inquiry. *Science and Children* 46 (2): 26–29.

Bell, R. L., L. Smetana, and I. Binns. 2005. Simplifying inquiry instruction. *The Science Teacher* 72 (7): 30–33.

Colburn, A. 2000. An inquiry primer. *Science Scope* 23 (6): 42–44.

Dochy, F., M. Segers, and M. M. Buehl. 1999. The relation between assessment practices and outcomes of studies: The case of research on prior knowledge. *Review of Educational Research* 69 (2): 145–186.

Herron, M. D. 1971. The nature of scientific enquiry. *The School Review* 79 (2): 171–212.

Langer, J. A. 1984. Examining background knowledge and text comprehension. *Reading Research Quarterly* 19 (4): 468–481.

Lee, O., S. Fradd, X. Sutman, and M. K. Saxton. 2001. Promoting science literacy with English language learners through instructional materials development: A case study. *Bilingual Research Journal* 25 (4): 479–501.

Llewellyn, D. 2005. *Teaching high school science through inquiry: A case study approach.* Thousand Oaks, CA: Corwin Press.

Marzano, R. 2004. *Building background knowledge for academic achievement: Research on what works in schools.* Alexandria, VA: Association for Supervision and Curriculum Development.

Marzano, R. 2006. *Classroom assessment and grading that work.* Alexandria, VA: Association for Supervision and Curriculum Development.

McComas, W. 2005. Laboratory instruction in the service of science teaching and learning: Reinventing and reinvigorating the laboratory experience. *The Science Teacher* 72 (7): 24–29.

Oleck, J. 2006. Is homework necessary? SLJ talks to Alfie Kohn. *School Library Journal. www.schoollibraryjournal.com/article/CA6397407.html.*

Stevens, K. C. 1980. The effect of background knowledge on the reading comprehension of ninth graders. *Journal of Reading Behavior* 12 (2): 151–154.

WARNING!

KEEP OUT OF REACH OF SMALL CHILDREN. KEEP THE LID ATTACHED FIRMLY AT ALL TIMES AND THE BOX ON A HIGH SHELF. CHOKING AND SWALLOWING HAZARDS FOR SMALL CHILDREN CONTAINED INSIDE.

WARNING!

KEEP OUT OF REACH OF SMALL CHILDREN. KEEP THE LID ATTACHED FIRMLY AT ALL TIMES AND THE BOX ON A HIGH SHELF. CHOKING AND SWALLOWING HAZARDS FOR SMALL CHILDREN CONTAINED INSIDE.

WARNING!

KEEP OUT OF REACH OF SMALL CHILDREN. KEEP THE LID ATTACHED FIRMLY AT ALL TIMES AND THE BOX ON A HIGH SHELF. CHOKING AND SWALLOWING HAZARDS FOR SMALL CHILDREN CONTAINED INSIDE.

WARNING!

KEEP OUT OF REACH OF SMALL CHILDREN. KEEP THE LID ATTACHED FIRMLY AT ALL TIMES AND THE BOX ON A HIGH SHELF. CHOKING AND SWALLOWING HAZARDS FOR SMALL CHILDREN CONTAINED INSIDE.

PLEASE DO NOT WRITE IN THIS MANUAL OR TEAR PAGES OUT OF IT. ALL OF YOUR INFORMATION GOES IN YOUR LAB NOTEBOOK. YOU MAY BE CHARGED FOR DAMAGE TO THIS BOOKLET JUST LIKE A LIBRARY BOOK.

You will be given extra copies of pages that need to be cut out or written on.

SECTION 1:

Science Process Skills, Measurement, and Scientific Inquiry

ACTIVITY 1: SCAVENGER HUNT

Objective

Students identify the scientific names of items they have around the house.

Purpose

Students will learn where they can go if they have a question about chemistry throughout the year and to preview some of the concepts they will learn.

The Scavenger Hunt is an activity that I refer to throughout the year. When I cover density, I will ask, "Who remembers in the Scavenger Hunt what item they chose for an object with a density of less than 1.0 g/ml? How did you know?" It helps level the background-knowledge playing field. I will be honest—it takes quite a bit of time to grade these projects, but it is well worth it for all the learning that comes of it. I gave students about a week to complete the project. It is impossible to allow students to work together on this assignment and still be able to tell who just gave answers without explanation. As such, I was never able to figure out a way to allow collaboration without allowing cheating on this activity. I made two slightly different versions of the same scavenger hunt to discourage blatant copying. One will say, "the distance from the sun to Venus," and the other will say, "the distance from the sun to Jupiter." A handful of students may have one version of the assignment and the answer to the other version.

Over the years, I have added more scavenger hunts. I gave out the version featured in the student section on the first day of school. Then, two weeks later, students received a metric system scavenger hunt in which they had to measure a variety of objects around their home and convert the measurements to metric units. When I realized that students could not remember from middle school the differences between an element, a compound, and a mixture, I gave an element hunt, which is described below. After the midterm, I would give another scavenger hunt with second-semester topics on it, such as acids and bases, gas laws, and organic chemistry.

Below are some variations of the scavenger hunts. Feel free to mix and match the additional items listed (pp. 4–5) and to add the element hunt or metric system scavenger hunt to your list of activities. You can change the rules as you please to allow a partner if you so desire or to change the way the activity is graded. I did not want to turn this into an internet scavenger hunt for which students bring pictures of items, so I required them to bring in actual items (with the exception of the metric system scavenger hunt). I believe that searching for an item and holding it in one's hand will increase the learning beyond doing an internet search for someone else's photograph. But teachers are free to set up and grade the scavenger hunts how they please.

To allow for the possibility that students may not have access to all of these items at home, I made it possible for a student to achieve a 100% score on this assignment without finding every single item. For example, in the scavenger hunt in the student manual, to get 100%, students only need to find 17 of the 20 items.

Additional Scavenger Hunt Items

- Something containing sulfur
- A polymer of ethylene terephthalate
- A newspaper article with a chemistry theme
- A picture of a scientist from the same country that your family comes from
- Metric container with the SI unit for volume
- Something with an alcohol group in it
- Something with an ester group in it
- Something with a pressure greater than 2.0 atm
- Something with a pressure less than 1.0 atm
- A proton donor
- A solution with the solute and solvent identified (e.g., "This is _____. The solute is _____ and the solvent is _____.")
- Something that could be separated through the process of distillation
- Result of a chemical change
- Allotropic form of carbon
- An ionic compound
- Sample of something ductile
- Sample of elemental Al
- Sample of elemental zinc
- Sample of a hydrocarbon
- 2-propanol
- An aromatic compound (not the common usage of *aromatic*, the chemistry usage)
- A liquid that has alum in it
- A volatile liquid
- 4 different crystalline substances
- Something with L-carvone or D-carvone in it
- A cardboard cube constructed to have the same volume as 0.10 mole of a gas at STP
- A non-electrolyte that dissolves in water
- A list of three ways to make a sugar cube dissolve faster

- Something containing potassium
- A covalent molecule
- A polymer
- A hydrated crystal
- Methyl salicylate
- Sample of elemental iron
- Sample of something brittle
- An electrolyte
- An electrical insulator
- Substance with a pH of 7 (other than water)
- Substance with a specific gravity less than 1
- A source of calcium
- Substance containing a halogen
- Substance that dissolves exothermically
- A solid solution
- A base
- Food source of boron (label and picture)
- A catalyst
- Something paramagnetic
- Sucrose
- Carbon dioxide
- A voltaic cell
- An oxygen-containing substance
- A non-aqueous solvent
- A substance with a boiling point below that of water
- An example of a colloidal suspension
- A mixture that could be separated by paper chromatography
- A volatile liquid
- A product containing an element with ___ protons (*Note:* For this item, choose an element that can be found in household products, such as iron [26], aluminum [13], or zinc [30].)
- Something containing a transition element from period 6
- A nonmetal
- 6.02×10^{23} of anything

Metric System Scavenger Hunt

Find as many of the following items as possible in the units given. Each item is worth 2 points, for a possible 50 points. The assignment is worth 40 points, so you only need 20 items to get full credit. For each item, show your work and include the source of the answer if necessary. Do not get help from other students. This is not a partner project, but an individual one. If you need to use measuring equipment, you should bring the object to class to measure.

Example

- The volume of a baseball in cm^3
- Diameter of baseball = 6 cm, radius = 3 cm
- Volume of a sphere = $4/3\pi r^3$ = $4/3\pi(3)^3$ = 113 cm^3

1. The volume of 25 pennies in cm^3 (and how you found it)
2. The length of the longest part of your hair in millimeters
3. The length of a teacher's pinky finger (not mine) in meters. Give the name of the teacher.
4. Something besides a meterstick that is between 97 and 103 cm
5. The height of the ceiling in this room in millimeters and how you figured it out
6. The distance from Mars to the Sun in kilometers, and where you found it
7. The mass of a brand-new yellow #2 wooden pencil in decigrams
8. The volume of a pack of 3 × 5 in. cards in cubic centimeters
9. The mass of a dollar in change in kilograms and the coins you used
10. The diameter of a compact disc in millimeters
11. The maximum volume of water that you can hold in your mouth, in milliliters
12. The number of milliliters in a 2-liter bottle
13. The mass of the Earth in grams, and where you found the information
14. The mass of meat (before cooking) in a McDonald's Quarter Pounder in grams (no, you do not need to buy one)
15. The number of cubic centimeters in a cubic meter
16. The mass in grams of 50.0 ml of water
17. The height of a counselor in meters, and the name of the counselor
18. The deepest depth of the ocean in kilometers (tell where you found the figure and the name of the area)
19. The number of nanoseconds in a second
20. The length of an assistant principal's shoe in centimeters, and the name of the assistant principal
21. The freezing point of water in degrees Celsius
22. The distance between George Washington's eyes on the one-dollar bill, in millimeters
23. The thickness of 1,000 chemistry books in kilometers, and how you figured it out
24. The length of a family member's car in meters, and what kind of car it is
25. How many songs can a 60 gigabyte MP3 player hold if each song is 4,000 bytes?

Topic: Element Names
Go to: *www.scilinks.org*
Code: THC01

Element Hunt

In this project, you will collect as many pure elements as you can. You will put all the elements you find on a poster board or cardboard labeled with what they are and where they came from if it is not obvious. The element must be nearly pure and in element form. For example, do not bring a car battery because it has sulfur in it.

Also, do not bring in carbon dioxide because it has carbon in it. Neither of these examples is in element form. The elements can be in a container if necessary. (*Note:* The first time I did the element hunt, students outsmarted me and brought in 25 items and made me pick out the 8 elements as I was grading them because there was no penalty for wrong answers. After that, I changed the grading system to penalize wrong answers to prevent this. It is described below.) For each item that you get correct, you get 5 points. For each item that you get wrong, you lose 4 points. So if you get 4 correct and 2 wrong, you get 12 points. That's not good.

The grading scale is as follows:

- 8 correct pure elements A+
- 7 elements B+
- 6 elements C+
- 5 elements D+
- < 5 elements F

Rules
1. If there is anything valuable, you can come back after school and pick it up.
2. Bring in the smallest amount possible.
3. Guessing is not a good idea.
4. Do not ask any other students for help on this. If you do, both of you will get a zero!
5. The element must be pure, not just a part of the product. Carbon dioxide is *not* carbon.

Safety
Some elements found in the home are too hazardous to be handled and should not be used. Examples include mercury, magnesium, and lead.

Scavenger Hunt Answers
Below are the answers to the scavenger hunt in the student manual.

1. Anything that has rusted or burned. Be open-minded about objects such as batteries that undergo redox reactions as they are used.
2. The metalloids are boron, silicon, germanium, arsenic, antimony, tellurium, and polonium. Generally, students bring a transistor, IC, or computer chip for silicon (silicone does not count) or a diode for germanium. This is one of the more difficult items.
3. Baking soda
4. PVC pipe and many plastics
5. Helium is the most common, but lightbulbs also are brought in and contain inert gases. Most "neon" lights do not have neon in them, so you can decide if you want to give credit for it.
6. Any dairy product, most vegetables, multivitamins, etc.

7. Sand, quartz, or glass; not silicone (bathtub sealer)
8. A battery
9. Mayonnaise, many hand lotions. Oil and water without an emulsifier does not count.
10. Any electrolyte, usually salt
11. Stainless steel, 14 K gold, sterling silver, brass, bronze, etc.
12. A base or alkaline substance such as soap or baking soda
13. Anything that sinks in water—e.g., rock, bolt, battery
14. Any molecule that does not dissolve in water, oil, sand, plastic, wood
15. Vinegar
16. A mixture that is constant throughout, fruit drinks, ketchup, air, coffee, etc.
17. Sugar and salt
18. Anything with iron in it, nail, screw, metals that stick to a magnet, some breakfast cereals
19. Most colored plants, rose petals, red cabbage, radishes
20. Answers will vary.

ACTIVITY 2: BUILDING YOUR BALANCE

Objective
Students learn how to use a single-beam balance to determine the masses of objects. Students use the density of water to determine the mass needed to balance the objects.

Purpose
Students will practice using their balances to hone their skills for future labs.

Materials
2 small cups (preferably plastic), plastic ruler, pencil, penny, nickel, dime, quarter

Notes
These balances are surprisingly accurate when used properly. Students should be given the accepted masses of the coins after the lab to determine if they measured properly. They should also be instructed to read the syringe to at least one decimal place. Using a hexagonal pencil will hurt their accuracy a bit, but using a round pencil makes it difficult to get stable balance. There are numerous designs for homemade single-beam balances; feel free to substitute another design if you prefer.

- Penny: 3.1 g before 1982, 2.5 g after
- Nickel: 4.95 g
- Dime: 2.25 g
- New state quarter: 5.68 g

Post-Lab Questions
1. Answers vary.
2. Answers vary but should include the balance shifted, the apparatus would not balance completely, etc.
3. Theoretically, one drop of water; realistically, around the mass of the dime

Topic: Density of Water
Go to: *www.scilinks.org*
Code: THC02

ACTIVITY 3: PENDULUM LAB

Objective
Students determine which of three variables affects the period of a pendulum.

Purpose
Students must isolate and test one variable at a time to be able to determine the proper variable. Students also practice other principles of good science. Although this seems like a physics lab, it is one of the only activities that allows three-variable manipulation and has the added bonus that most students do not know the answer; another benefit is that it can be done with simple materials.

Materials
Thread or dental floss, washers, a timer

Notes
Contrary to the popular misconception, the only variable that affects the period of the pendulum is the length of the string (when used at small angles). If students do not raise the angle too high, angle and mass make no measurable difference. Students must be warned that a change from 1.20 to 1.22 seconds is not significant. They must be instructed to keep everything else constant, such as timing strategy, swinging method, counting method, and number of swings. When you assess this assignment and provide feedback, you should see if students held two variables constant as they tested the other (e.g., held the length and angle constant when testing the mass).

Post-Lab Questions
1. Length
2. Swings of the same length swing at the same speed regardless of the size of the person on the swing or how high the swing is going. Swings of different lengths swing out of sync.

Topic: Pendulums
Go to: *www.scilinks.org*
Code: THC03

3. Graphs will vary, but two examples are below. Teachers may give as much or as little guidance for the graphs as they choose. The type of graph (line, bar, etc.) is not critical.

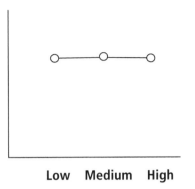

Low Medium High

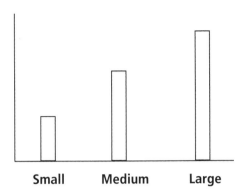

Small Medium Large

ACTIVITY 4: THICKNESS OF PAPER LAB

Objective
Students determine the thickness of one sheet of paper.

Purpose
Students learn the difference between a measured value and a calculated value. Students learn to measure and calculate using the metric system and very small numbers. Students are prepared for other similar labs used in chemistry classes, such as Oleic Acid lab and Thickness of Aluminum Foil lab. Students learn how to determine how many decimal places to include in a measurement.

Materials
Ruler, neat stack of paper

Notes
This is the perfect example of an activity that can be assigned at a number of different levels of inquiry. If the teacher chooses to do so, the instructions may be removed and the inquiry level of the activity increased. The teacher may also choose to assign the activity before discussing measuring by grouping. Or, in certain circumstances, the teacher may give the step-by-step instructions included in the student portion. For most of the activities, full instructions are given and the teacher may choose to leave them out to assign an inquiry activity.

Answers vary on this lab for many reasons. First, the thickness of paper varies. Also, some students do not flatten the stack of paper all the way. Encourage students to take their measurements out to the correct number of decimal places and measure in centimeters or meters. Give students an accepted value for typing paper with which they can compare their answers. The website at *www.paper-paper.com/weight.html* has an excellent chart with paper thicknesses. A fairly common paper size is 24 bond with a thickness of 0.00012 m. Students who measure to the correct decimal place usually get between 0.00011 and 0.00014. It is much more likely they will get an answer that is too large rather than too small.

Topic: SI Measurement
Go to: *www.scilinks.org*
Code: THC04

Post-Lab Questions

1. Air between papers, extra material on the end of the ruler, thickness of the lines on the ruler, wrinkled papers, etc.
2. Answers vary, but approximately 120 m.
3. Answers vary, but approximately 25,400.
4. Answers vary. Use the internet value if you do not have a micrometer.

ACTIVITY 5: GRAPHING THE BALL'S BOUNCE

Objective
Students measure the height of a ball's bounce versus its drop height.

Purpose
Students get practice measuring, averaging, and calculating metric values. Students practice setting up graphs and graphing laboratory data.

Materials
Rubber ball, ruler

Notes
Encourage students to do graphs that fill up a whole page so meaningful data can be extrapolated from the graph. Also, discourage the practice of just putting the data on the axes and getting a straight line. I found that many students coming into my class, when asked to graph the pairs [(0, 2), (1, 6), (3, 18)], would simply put 0, 1, and 3 on the x-axis and 2, 6, and 18 on the y-axis (evenly spaced) and draw a straight line through the points. Many students do not know how to graph data collected in science classes because it involves calculating what scale to use and graphing numbers that are not always nice and round.

There is a demonstration available from many science equipment distributors called Happy and Sad Balls that would be a fun demonstration to go along with this activity. Although the balls look and feel exactly the same, one bounces and the other does not.

Topic: Measurements and Data
Go to: *www.scilinks.org*
Code: THC05

Post-Lab Questions
1. Answers vary between straight and downward trending. Most balls get less efficient the higher they go. But students might not reach that height in this activity, so straight is an acceptable answer as well.
2. Yes, it is legitimate because if you drop it from 0 cm, it will bounce 0 cm.
3. Answers vary, but likely between 100 and 175 cm
4. Answers vary, but likely between 8 and 14 cm

ACTIVITY 6: INVESTIGATING AN URBAN LEGEND

Objective
Students test the idea that gravity makes you shorter from morning to night.

Purpose
Students practice making measurements and performing calculations in the metric system, as well as controlling all variables except the one being tested.

Materials
Pencil, ruler

Notes
Students must measure accurately or they will get bad results. Some have even concluded that they got taller throughout the day because they were not careful with their measurements.

Post-Lab Questions
1. Yes, in most cases, students find that they get a little bit shorter.
2. Gravity compresses the disks in the spine. A student could stay in bed for a few hours on a Saturday and see if it makes a difference.
3. Yes, they would work, but only temporarily.

Topic: Force of Gravity
Go to: *www.scilinks.org*
Code: THC06

ACTIVITY 7: THE MOLE

Objective
Students will describe a mole of different substances.

Purpose
Students will practice calculating the mass and/or volume of a mole of different substances and will become familiar with the idea that a mole of different substances represents different masses and volumes of those substances.

Materials
Balance, pre-1982 pennies, water, sand, baking soda

Notes
For many substances, a mole is a large amount of the substance. For substances such as vegetable oil and sugar, students may measure a small fraction of a mole and then imagine what a full mole would look like. Their balances are not capable of measuring a full mole of sugar.

Post-Lab Questions
1. 360 tablets
2. Potassium chloride because potassium has a higher molar mass than sodium
3. A mixture does not have a definite composition, so every mixture would have a different molar mass depending on the proportions of the components.

Topic: The Mole
Go to: *www.scilinks.org*
Code: THC07

ACTIVITY 8: CALCULATING MOLES LAB

Objective
Students calculate how many moles of salt and sugar are contained in packets.

Purpose
Students practice using their balances and converting from grams to moles using the periodic table.

Materials
2 salt packets, sugar packet, balance (from Activity 2)

Notes
Get the largest salt packets you can find or give students two packets. One packet may be too small to be weighed with these balances. Every packet varies slightly in its weight, so teachers must find the mass of the packets on a balance to check the answers and should be flexible in accepting answers.

Post-Lab Questions
1. Answers may vary but students should see that there were more moles of salt in the smaller packet due to the large molar mass of sugar.
2. Answers will vary, but students should multiply the molar mass of sugar by the number of moles of salt.
3. Answers will vary. My classes generally come up with a density of sugar around 2.5–3.0 g/cm^3. The approximate density of salt is 2.2 g/cm^3 and the answers varied between 1.4 and 2.0. Because the densities are so close, students should not be graded on their answer, but instead on their measuring, calculating, and estimating skills. Also, the grain size of the crystals affects the answer, but the grain sizes of commercial salt and sugar are similar.

ACTIVITY 1: SCAVENGER HUNT

QUESTION ?

Where can you find unknown chemistry information when questions arise throughout the year?

SAFETY

Do not bring any flammables, explosives, pesticides, concentrated cleaners, pharmaceuticals, poisonous substances, or illegal objects to school. Use goggles if collecting materials that may harm your eyes.

Guidelines

1. Each item must have a label with a description of its contents and the number of the item from the list that it represents (e.g., Table Salt #33). All solid substances should be put in a plastic bag or plastic wrap. All liquids should be in plastic or glass containers with tight, sealable lids. Put all items in a box with your name on it. Do not include large amounts of substances; a spoonful of powders or liquids is enough.
2. Each item collected correctly is worth 3 points, for a possible total of 60 points. The assignment is worth 51 points, so there is the possibility of getting 9 extra credit points. You only need 17 correct items to get full credit.
3. You may ask anyone for help on this except other chemistry or physics students. Most of the items have many correct answers, so copying will be obvious. If you copy, you will both receive a score of zero. THIS IS NOT A PARTNER PROJECT!

List

1. A product that has experienced an oxidation-reduction (redox) reaction
2. A metalloid
3. Sodium bicarbonate
4. A polymer of vinyl chloride
5. An inert gas (also known as a noble gas)
6. A source of calcium
7. SiO_2
8. An electrochemical cell
9. An emulsion (not just a mixture)
10. Something that lowers the freezing point of water
11. An alloy (not metal plated)
12. A substance with a pH greater than 7.0
13. A substance with a density greater than 1.0 g/ml
14. Something with nonpolar molecules
15. Acetic acid
16. A homogeneous substance (not homogenized)
17. A substance with a solubility of more than 300 g/L at room temperature
18. A product containing an element with 26 protons
19. An acid-base indicator
20. A picture of a famous female chemist

ACTIVITY 2: BUILDING YOUR BALANCE

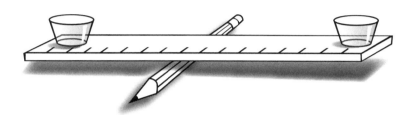

QUESTION ?

How does a single-beam balance work?

SAFETY

Use only clean water in your syringe. Slowly push the plunger to avoid splashing the water. Never work near an electrical outlet or source. Clean up any spills when finished to avoid slips and falls.

MATERIALS

2 small cups (preferably plastic), plastic ruler, pencil, penny, nickel, dime, quarter

PROCEDURE

You will need a simple balance for many of the activities in this book. To build your balance, you will put a cup on each end of the ruler and balance the ruler on a pencil or pen placed under the middle of the ruler. Attach the cups with tape or glue, then make adjustments in the balance point by adding small extra pieces of tape or clay until the ruler is balanced. When balanced, the ruler may not be perfectly level, but you will be able to tell that tapping it can cause it to sway to either side. When the ruler is not balanced, it will only sway to one side. You should check the empty balance point before each time you use it and make adjustments as necessary. The object that you want to find the mass of should be put in one cup, then you can use the syringe to fill the other cup with water until you have a balance, recording in your lab notebook the beginning and ending volumes in the syringe. Make sure that your balance is on a flat table with both cups over the table. If one side gets too heavy, you do not want the whole balance to fall on the floor.

Remember that the density of water is 1.0 g/ml. That means that 1 ml of water has a mass of 1 g. If it takes 27 ml of water to balance out the sample, then the mass of the sample is 27 g.

This is just one type of simple balance. Other balances might hang from a string or involve other methods. If this one does not work well for you, investigate other methods online and build another type of balance. As long as the balance has a beam that can be balanced with water, it will be fine for all of these activities.

Testing Your Balance

Test your balance by finding the masses of four different coins, and record those masses below. The accepted masses will be given to you by your teacher to ensure that you use the balance correctly.

Data

Mass of penny _____ g
Date on penny _____

Mass of nickel _____ g

Mass of dime _____ g

Mass of quarter _____ g

Post-Lab Questions

1. What was the percentage difference between your measurement and the accepted mass (as provided by your teacher)? Percent difference = ([difference between the two answers] ÷ [accepted answer]) × 100
2. What do you think was the biggest contributor to that difference?
3. What do you think is the lightest mass that you could find using this balance?

ACTIVITY 3: PENDULUM LAB

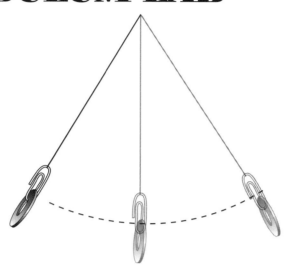

QUESTION ❓

Which variables affect the period of a pendulum?

SAFETY

Do not swing the pendulum in a dangerous manner. Washers can be a choking hazard, so keep them out of the reach of children.

MATERIALS

Thread or dental floss, washers, a timer

PROCEDURE

In this lab, you will determine which of three factors determines the period of a pendulum. A pendulum is a weight hanging from a string. You will use a piece of thread or dental floss (approximately 50 cm) and washers to make your pendulum. The period is how long it takes the pendulum to swing back and forth once. The three factors, or variables, that you will test are the mass at the end of the pendulum, the angle from which the pendulum is dropped, and the length of the pendulum. You need to follow the rules of a good experiment (i.e., changing only one variable at a time, repeating each trial more than once, etc.). This procedure will mainly be determined by you, but here are some tips:

1. Do not swing the pendulum from high angles (greater than 35°), or it will not swing smoothly.
2. It will be nearly impossible to measure one swing of the pendulum accurately; you will want to let the pendulum swing multiple times and then divide the total number of swings.
3. You do not have to measure the exact masses, angles, and lengths of the pendulum. You can use low, medium, and high angles; short, medium, and long lengths; and one, two, and three washers.
4. If one or more of the factors does affect the period of the pendulum, it will affect it greatly. Do not let periods of 1.21 and 1.23 sec. make you think there was a change. The difference will be more like periods of 1.21 and 3.23 sec.

Data

Because you will determine the procedure, you also will determine the data charts. Keep in mind that you should test each variable (length, angle, and mass) at three different levels (low, medium, and high).

Post-Lab Questions

1. Which variable or variables had the biggest effect on the period of the pendulum?
2. Can you relate this information to your experiences on or around playground swings? Explain.
3. Draw three line graphs or bar graphs. Each graph should have the variable being tested on the x-axis and the period on the y-axis. Start the y-axis at 0 to avoid amplifying small changes.

ACTIVITY 4: THICKNESS OF PAPER LAB

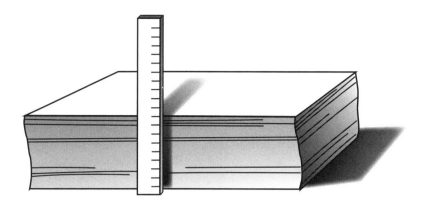

QUESTION ❓

How thick is a sheet of paper?

SAFETY 🩹

Put the lid back on the box and keep the box out of the reach of children.

MATERIALS 📏

Ruler, neat stack of paper

PROCEDURE 👣

Scientists have measured objects that seem impossible to measure. We know the diameter of a proton, the speed of light, and the size of the visible universe. Each is impossible to measure directly, so scientists have developed ingenious methods for measuring them indirectly. It would be impossible to accurately measure the thickness of one sheet of paper with a ruler. In this lab, you will measure a stack of paper and mathematically determine the thickness of one sheet of paper.

This is similar to calculations you will do later in chemistry. It would be impossible for us to directly measure the mass of one atom of carbon. We can, however, find the mass of a large number of carbon atoms and then figure out the mass of a single atom. The quantity of atoms that we use is the mole. The mole is the number of atoms that have a mass (in grams) equal to the atomic mass found on the periodic table. For example, an atom of carbon has a mass of 12.011 atomic mass units (amu). A mole of carbon has a mass of 12.011 g.

Take a large number of papers (e.g., 100, 250, or 500; preferably new papers that have not yet been bent or crinkled) and measure the thickness of the stack. Be sure to measure in centimeters. Even though most rulers have "mm" on the side of the ruler that goes from 1 to 30, those are actually the number of centimeters.

Data

Number of sheets of paper _____

Thickness of the stack _____ cm

Thickness of one sheet _____ cm

Post-Lab Questions

1. What were some sources of error in this lab?
2. How tall would a stack of 1,000,000 sheets of paper stand?
3. How many sheets of paper would it take to stand as tall as a basketball rim (10 ft)? (1 in. = 2.54 cm)
4. Your teacher will use a device called a micrometer to actually measure a piece of paper. Calculate the percentage difference by using the following equation:

$$\text{Percentage difference} = \frac{(\text{difference between your calculation and the teacher's measurement})}{(\text{teacher's actual measurement})} \times 100$$

ACTIVITY 5: GRAPHING THE BALL'S BOUNCE

QUESTION ❓

How efficient is a bouncing rubber ball?

SAFETY

Rubber balls and marbles are choking and slip-and-fall hazards.

MATERIALS

Rubber ball, ruler

PROCEDURE

In this lab, you will practice your graphing and measuring skills by preparing a graph of the relationship between the height from which a ball is dropped and how high it bounces. You will try to determine if there is a regular percentage of the height that it always bounces, or if it bounces a larger or smaller percentage of the height as the drop height is increased. If you drop the ball from a particular height and measure how high it bounces, the percent difference between those two numbers can be called the efficiency of the bounce. For example, if you drop the ball from 100 cm and it bounces back 80 cm, then it has an efficiency of 80%.

Data

Drop Height (cm)	Bounce Height Trial 1	Bounce Height Trial 2	Bounce Height Trial 3	Average Bounce Height
30				
40				
50				
60				
70				
80				
90				
100				

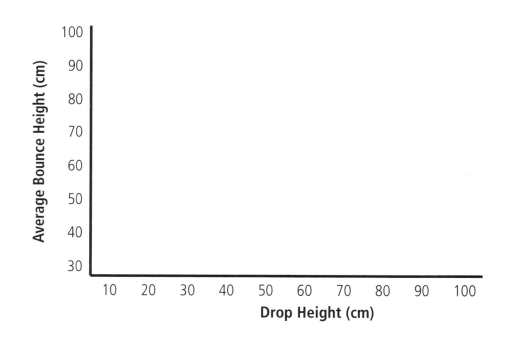

1. Use a ruler to put marks on a wall or other vertical surface up to 100 cm. Do not write on the wall; use sticky notes or tape.
2. Drop the ball from different heights (30, 40, 50, 60, 70, 80, 90, and 100 cm) and measure how high it bounces after each drop. Repeat this three times and average your results for each height. You may measure from the top or bottom of the ball, but you should be consistent.
3. Prepare a graph with drop height on the *x*-axis and average bounce height on the *y*-axis.

Post-Lab Questions

1. What can you say about the shape of your graph? Was it flat, upward trending, downward trending, or random? What does the pattern mean about the bounce of the ball?
2. On some graphs, the point (0,0) is a legitimate point, and on some graphs it is not. Is that point legitimate on this graph? If so, start your line there. If not, start it at the first data point.
3. If the pattern continued in this way, what would the bounce height be if the drop height is 200 cm?
4. What would the bounce height be if the drop height is 15 cm?

ACTIVITY 6: INVESTIGATING AN URBAN LEGEND

QUESTION ❓

Are you taller in the morning than at night?

SAFETY 🩹

Keep the sealed box of materials out of the reach of children. Your partner should not stand on an unstable object if he or she is shorter than you.

MATERIALS 📏

Pencil, ruler

PROCEDURE 👣

In this lab, you will investigate what may possibly be an urban legend. Some say that when you wake up in the morning, you are taller than you are later in the day. You will test this theory by measuring your height as soon as you get up in the morning and then again at the end of the day. The difference, if any, will be small, so it is important that you control all possible variables and measure as accurately as possible.

1. Be sure that your shoes are off and you are standing on level ground. Have someone mark your height with a small mark on a wall or doorway, making sure that the pencil is completely level. This is easier if the other person is taller than you. Do not make permanent marks on the wall—use a light pencil mark or tape.
2. Use your ruler to measure carefully the height of the mark from the floor.
3. Repeat this procedure again at the end of the day. Measure carefully. If there is an effect, it will be a small one.
4. Repeat the procedure on several days and try to find other volunteers to do the same.

Data

Height in the morning: _____ cm

Height in the evening: _____ cm

Post-Lab Questions

1. Is it true that you get shorter later in the day? Explain how you came to this conclusion.
2. How would you explain this phenomenon if it is true? How could you test your hypothesis?
3. Devices to hang upside-down from your ankles used to be popular for relieving pressure in your spine. Could this possibly work? Will it make you taller in the long run? Explain.

ACTIVITY 7: THE MOLE

QUESTION ❓

What does a mole of different substances look like?

SAFETY

Baking soda can harm your eyes. Wear goggles during this activity. Dispose of all chemicals, clean up all spills, and wash your hands when finished.

MATERIALS

Balance, pre-1982 pennies, water, sand, baking soda

PROCEDURE

Because atoms and molecules are so small, chemists created a quantity called a mole that represents a large number of atoms. The unit of a mole is like a dozen in that it represents a certain number of atoms or molecules. It is a very, very, very large number but the same idea as a pair, a dozen, a gross, and so on. A pair is 2 items, a dozen is 12 items, a gross is 144 items, and a mole is 6.0×10^{23} items. That is 600,000,000,000,000,000,000,000 items in a mole. But what does a mole of a substance look like? You will find out in this activity.

   In this activity, you will use your balance to measure out approximately 1 mole of different substances. Recall from the experiment where you built your balance that the density of water is 1.0 g/ ml. Therefore, 1 ml of water has a mass of 1 g. You will use this information and the periodic table to determine how much of each substance composes a mole.

The periodic table tells you the mass of a mole of each element. For example, the mass of a mole of carbon is 12.011 g. To find the mass of a compound, you simply add up the masses of each element that makes up that compound. For example, a mole of calcium carbonate ($CaCO_3$) would have a mass of approximately 100 g (40.078 + 12.011 + 3[15.999] = 100.086). Your balance is not sensitive enough to measure the 0.086 grams, so for take-home labs we will just ignore that part and round it to 100 g.

Use your balance, the periodic table, and the known density of water to determine 1 mole of the following items. Describe how much of each makes up 1 mole (e.g., seven and a half pennies, a large handful of sand). If a mole of the substance is very large, you may measure half a mole or one-tenth of a mole and then describe what a full mole would look like.

Substance	Number of Grams	Description
Pennies (Pre-1982 pennies are pure copper and post-1982 pennies are not, so use pre-1982 pennies.)		
Water (H_2O)		
Sand (Pure sand is SiO_2; assume that your sand is pure.)		
Baking soda (sodium bicarbonate, $NaHCO_3$)		

Post-Lab Questions

1. How many 500 mg aspirin tablets would it take to make a mole of aspirin ($C_9H_8O_4$)?
2. Which would be heavier, a mole of sodium chloride or a mole of potassium chloride? Explain.
3. Why can you not determine the mass of a mole of most mixtures?

Extension

It has been said that there are more molecules of SiO_2 in a grain of sand than there are grains of sand on an entire beach. Estimate the size of a grain of sand to determine approximately how many molecules of SiO_2 are in the grain. You may have to look up more information, such as the density of sand and/or the mass of SiO_2, to make this estimate.

ACTIVITY 8: CALCULATING MOLES LAB

QUESTION

How many moles of sugar and salt are contained in a packet of salt or sugar?

SAFETY

Dispose of each material after use; do not use the salt or sugar on your food. Clean up any spills and dispose of all chemicals when finished.

MATERIALS

2 salt packets, sugar packet, balance (from Activity 2)

PROCEDURE

In this lab, you will use your balance to calculate how many moles of salt are in a packet of salt and how many moles of sugar are in a packet of sugar.

1. Pour the contents of the sugar packet completely into one of the cups on your balance.
2. Find the mass of the sugar and record it below.
3. Repeat this procedure with the salt. Use two salt packets since they are so small.

Data

Mass of sugar _____ g

Mass of 2 salt packets _____ g

Calculations

Using the formulas for salt (NaCl) and sugar ($C_6H_{12}O_6$) now calculate how many moles of each were in the packets.

Moles of salt _____ moles

Moles of sugar _____ moles

Post-Lab Questions

1. Which packet was bigger? Which packet had more moles in it? Explain.
2. How many grams of sugar would it take to make the same number of moles as the salt?
3. Estimating the volume of the two packets (e.g., half as big as the other, twice as big) and considering their masses, which do you think is more dense, salt or sugar?

SECTION 2:
Chemical and Physical Properties

ACTIVITY 9: SOLUTIONS, SUSPENSIONS, AND MIXTURES

Objective

Students will test whether solutions, suspensions, and mixtures can be separated with a filter.

Purpose

It is a strong misconception among students that solutions can be separated with a filter. This activity is designed to address that misconception in preparation for the separation lab, in which they will have to figure out a way to separate salt from salt water. This activity will let them figure out that filtering will not work.

Materials

Salt or sugar, coffee filter, baby powder or cornstarch, sand or dirt, water, food coloring, baking soda, other food ingredients (for mixing)

Notes

Many students will be surprised that they cannot filter salt out of salt water, so in the follow-up discussion, make sure the misconception is gone and students do not try to justify holding onto misconceptions with excuses for why it did not work.

Post-Lab Questions

1. Solution: no; Suspension: yes; Mixture: yes
2. Soda is a solution; orange juice pulp is a mixture.
3. No, salt cannot simply be filtered out of salt water.

SC*L*INKS.
THE WORLD'S A CLICK AWAY

Topic: Mixtures and Pure Substances
Go to: *www.scilinks.org*
Code: THC08

ACTIVITY 10: SEPARATION LAB: ELEMENTS, COMPOUNDS, AND MIXTURES

Objective
Students will separate a mixture of sand, salt, Styrofoam (or Perlite), and iron.

Purpose
Students will use the physical and chemical properties of this mixture to separate it, thus proving that it is a mixture, not an element or compound.

Materials
Bag of mixture (see Preparation), an assortment of separating tools that will vary by student

Notes
Some teachers choose to perform some of these take-home activities in class. I would not recommend choosing this activity to be performed in the classroom. It is extremely time-consuming to clean up the resulting sand in the sinks and hundreds of evaporating dishes in the windows that must sit for several days to evaporate. It truly is best done at home. Some teachers prefer to have students plan a strategy and get it approved before starting. Allowing students to just go and investigate can cause them to make mistakes that will require a new bag of materials. Individuals may decide how they want to handle that.

The most efficient way to separate this mixture is to get the iron out with a magnet (before adding water). Then pour water and scoop the floating Styrofoam. Then pour off the salt water and evaporate it. Simply dry the sand.

Preparation
Teacher must prepare one zip-top bag of mixture for each student. The bags should be about 1 part iron filings, 1 part salt, 3 parts Perlite, and 25 parts sand. Students

Topic: Physical and Chemical Properties of Matter
Go to: *www.scilinks.org*
Code: THC09

turn in the separated substances in labeled zip-top bags. They should turn in all of the separated materials so the teacher can judge how well they were separated. Measuring spoons are great for mixing the substances in the bags.

Post-Lab Questions

1. Iron: magnetism; Styrofoam: density; Salt: soluble in water; Sand: chemically inert and density
2. This was a mixture because it was separated using only physical changes.
3. Answers will vary: ketchup, salsa, air, salt water, Kool-Aid, 14 K gold, etc.

Safety

Encourage students to not heat any liquids, but allow them to evaporate. Give students at least a week to perform this activity to allow for evaporation time. A student who plans ahead can complete the activity with dry salt and sand in one week.

ACTIVITY 11: PROBABILITY OF FINDING AN ELECTRON

Objective

Students will use a target to simulate the probability of finding an electron in a certain energy level.

Purpose

This activity will reinforce the idea of probability and help students realize that even if the probability of finding an electron is very high in one region, it is possible that the electron can still be found in other regions.

Materials

Pen or pencil, copy of target (p. 235)

Notes

A good point about statistics and trials may be made by collecting large numbers of student data and compiling them into one huge data set.

Post-Lab Questions

1. Answers will vary.
2. Answers will vary, but there should be one ring that was hit much more frequently than the others. It is usually close to the center but not at the center itself.
3. Although it would be more likely than the others, at any particular time, one cannot be sure exactly where it will land.

SCI LINKS.
THE WORLD'S A CLICK AWAY

Topic: The Electron
Go to: *www.scilinks.org*
Code: THC10

ACTIVITY 12: HALF-LIFE SIMULATION

Objective

Students will simulate the decay of radioactive isotopes by flipping papers and removing face-up papers.

Purpose

This activity will help students internalize the idea of half-life and the randomness of radioactive decay.

Materials

Copy of provided paper (p. 237), scissors, shoe box

Post-Lab Questions

1. Answers will vary, but should be around 6 or 7.
2. Answers will vary slightly, but should be around 1,000. Many students will think that the half-life is half the time it takes for all of the papers to be removed and will put 3,000 or 3,500. Be sure to correct this habit. An example of how students should figure out the half-life appears on page 50

Topic: Radioactive Decay
Go to: *www.scilinks.org*
Code: THC11

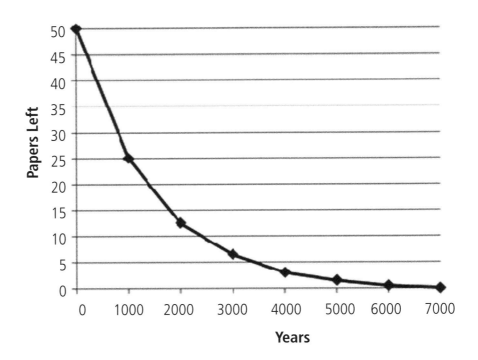

This is an example of how students will do it if they believe that half-life means half the time it takes for the particles to decay.

3. Answers will vary, but should be close to 2,000 years.
4. Answers will vary, but should be about 6,000 or 7,000 years.

ACTIVITY 13: RUTHERFORD'S GOLD FOIL SIMULATION

Objective
Students will simulate Rutherford's gold foil simulation by rolling a marble (alpha particle) at a series of target marbles (gold atoms).

Purpose
Students will visualize Rutherford's experiment and internalize the common phrase, "Atoms are mostly empty space."

Materials
Ruler, 6 marbles

Notes
If students are not random in their rolling of the marble, the answer will not come out well. If they have to stand facing away from the marbles or even kick the marble, it must be random. Answers should come out to about 20–30 hits out of 100 tries, depending on the diameter of the marbles used.

Post-Lab Questions
1. Answers will vary, but should be within 10% if the marble is thrown randomly.
2. Because Rutherford could not see the gold particles and aim at them. For probabilities to work, the event has to be completely random. Any aiming will make your answer too high.
3. Probabilities are also always based on a large number of trials. If you were to roll 4 times and hit twice, your answer would come out to be 2.5 cm, which is much too high.

Activity adapted from Robinson, P., and P. G. Hewitt. 1987. *Conceptual physics laboratory manual.* 8th ed. Menlo Park, CA: Addison-Wesley.

SCI**LINKS**
THE WORLD'S A CLICK AWAY
Topic: Structure of Atoms
Go to: *www.scilinks.org*
Code: THC12

ACTIVITY 14: MEAN FREE PATH ACTIVITY

Objective
Students will calculate the mean free path of a simulated gas sample.

Purpose
Students will internalize what mean free path is, visualize particles as being independent of each other in a gas or plasma, and practice measuring in metric units and calculating averages.

Topic: Gases
Go to: *www.scilinks.org*
Code: THC13

Materials
Ruler, target diagram (p. 118)

Note
It is important for students to measure from one atom to a neighboring atom, not one all the way across the circle.

Post-Lab Questions
1. No, it would not affect the final answer very much because it is the average of 10 measurements, so one measurement does not affect the average significantly.
2. Increasing the number would make them closer together, thus lowering the mean free path.
3. Increasing the size of the container would increase the mean free path because gases and plasmas fill their containers. The same number of particles in a larger container would be farther apart.

ACTIVITY 15: FREEZING WATER

Objective
Students will see if the volume of an ice and water mixture goes up or down when the ice melts.

Topic: Properties of Water
Go to: *www.scilinks.org*
Code: THC14

Purpose
Students will see that water expands as it freezes, thus lowering its density and causing it to float. Students also practice measuring volume in metric units.

Materials
Syringe, syringe cap, ice cube, water, pencil

Post-Lab Questions
1. Water level was higher before the ice melted.
2. Water expands when it freezes.
3. Because the liquid inside will expand and burst the sealed container
4. If the mass of the ice is the same and the volume gets smaller as it melts, the density of water is higher. That is why ice floats.

ACTIVITY 16: SURFACE TENSION LAB

Objective

Students will count how many drops of water they can put on the face of a penny with and without dishwashing liquid in the water.

Purpose

Students will observe the effect of surface tension on the properties of water.

Materials

Penny, water, syringe, dishwashing liquid

Post-Lab Questions

1. The water without dishwashing liquid allowed the most drops because dishwashing liquid reduces surface tension.
2. It would allow more drops because it would hold the water together more strongly.
3. Most students predict too low, less than 10 drops. If performed carefully, sometimes more than 40 drops can be added, depending on the age of the coin and the quality of the water.

ACTIVITY 17: DENSITY OF OIL LAB

Objective
Students will estimate the density of cooking oil by comparing it to water.

Purpose
Students will see the connection among mass, volume, and density by comparing the density of two substances with equal mass and unequal volumes. This activity helps them understand that density depends on both mass and volume when, intuitively, students only connect density with mass.

Materials
Cooking oil, dishwashing liquid, water, syringe, balance (Activity 2)

Notes
Students get surprisingly good results from this experiment. Because the density of store-bought oil varies, this is not a good lab to grade for accuracy. Grades should be based on calculations and post-lab questions.

Post-Lab Questions
1. Water is denser in nearly all cases.
2. Because oil is less dense, it takes a larger volume to make an equal mass.
3. Water is denser, so an equal volume of water will have a higher mass than oil.

Topic: Density
Go to: *www.scilinks.org*
Code: THC15

ACTIVITY 18: CHROMATOGRAPHY LAB

Objective
Students will perform paper chromatography on different inks to find the source of the ink.

Purpose
Students will see that different combinations of colors in the ink can make the same color ink and that some mixtures can be separated with chromatography. Different forms of chromatography are important in science research.

Materials
Coffee filter, drinking glasses, pencils, scissors

Notes
Black markers work well, as students will be surprised to find that they contain purple, yellow, and green, among other colors, in the ink. Overhead markers work best. If permanent markers are used, water may not be suitable for the solvent. Alcohol or acetone must be used.

Set up the crime scene by having the three or four markers in an official-looking envelope and each one labeled with the name of the former owner. I choose myself and other teachers or the principal as suspects to make the scene more interesting. Have students bring up their precut papers and put a mark from each marker on the paper. As they mark them, they can write the name of the suspect in pencil.

Prepare the evidence sample by running your own chromatogram and tear off a part of it that contains a color fairly unique to that marker. Do not make it too easy. Also, I try to choose one of the colors that will surprise students when they learn it came from a black marker, such as purple and yellow. Tape the evidence to the front desk so that students can compare their chromatograms to it.

SCiLINKS.
THE WORLD'S A CLICK AWAY

Topic: Chromatography
Go to: *www.scilinks.org*
Code: THC16

Post-Lab Questions

1. No, this could not be used alone to convict a criminal because there are usually numerous people in a city who use the same type of marker. But combined with other evidence, it can be powerful.
2. Answers will vary based on the markers used.
3. Usually if two yellow colors come out of different inks, they will have similar retention factors, but occasionally the same color can have a different chemical composition.

ACTIVITY 19: DENSITY COLUMN IN A STRAW

Objective

Students will make a series of liquid layers with different densities using nontoxic chemicals.

Purpose

Students will see how the amount of solute in a solution affects its density.

Materials

Sugar, water, transparent drinking straw, three small cups, food coloring or colored drinks (such as Kool-Aid or Gatorade)

Notes

A discussion of why the different liquids do not mix when the column is made is probably beyond comprehension for the average high school class. The solutions will mix if not handled gently. The same effect can be made in a large graduated cylinder as a demonstration in the class. Just fit a large funnel with a rubber tube and a pinchcock clamp (a spring-loaded device that will squeeze the rubber tube closed when you don't want liquid to flow). Starting with the densest solution, add each of the sugar solutions with a different color slowly down the side of the cylinder. Small objects such as corks, marbles, popcorn kernels, and marbles can be placed in the cylinder to see the layer on which they will float. You can test the floating objects in the prepared solutions before you put them in the cylinder. This is far safer than versions with mercury, mineral oil, and alcohols.

Post-Lab Questions

1. Warmer water will be on top because it expands as it warms and its density is lowered. In the winter in a calm lake, this effect can be reversed slightly as the surface of the water is cooled; it can stay at the surface until it freezes. Then it stays there because ice is less dense than water.

2. The freshwater will stay on the surface because it is less dense than the salt water. Eventually, it will mix with the salt water, but near the mouth of the river the layers are fairly distinct.

3. Water is denser. If one wanted to figure it out, one could just mix some oil and water and see which one floated to the top. The top one is less dense and the bottom is denser. Oil floats on water.

ACTIVITY 20: MECHANOLUMINESCENCE: MAKING THINGS LIGHT UP

Objective
Students will see how applying a force to a Wint-O-Green Life Saver causes it to light up.

Purpose
Students will understand that light (even invisible light) can be absorbed and re-emitted at a different wavelength or color. They will begin to connect colors of light with the electromagnetic spectrum.

Materials
Several Wint-O-Green Life Savers, transparent tape, 2 sugar cubes

Notes
This activity should be completed after students have been introduced to the electromagnetic spectrum in class. Have students try as many mechanoluminescent combinations as possible and comment on the color and whether that color was given off directly or absorbed and re-emitted.

Post-Lab Questions
1. Answers vary from blue to blue-green to green depending on the sensitivity of the eye and how long the eyes were allowed to adjust to the darkness. Because the eye is more sensitive to green, one who walks right in and performs the experiment will see green. The longer the eyes are allowed to adjust, the more blue one will see.
2. Blue-green or green.
3. a. Blue-violet
   b. Approximately 550 nm. No, because sugar would be closer to 400 nm and you would be able to smell wintergreen.
   c. Violet

Topic: Electromagnetic Spectrum
Go to: *www.scilinks.org*
Code: THC17

ACTIVITY 21: INTENSIVE AND EXTENSIVE PROPERTIES

Objective
Students will split colored water into different cups and observe the properties.

Purpose
Students will know that the properties that do not change when the liquid is split up are intensive and those that do change are extensive.

Materials
3 small cups, food coloring or colored drinks

Notes
Students have difficulty remembering whether a property is intensive or extensive if the differences are just presented in lecture form. A simple lab like this one can help them remember the differences longer. Using the terms repeatedly can also help students internalize them. The difference here is that intensive properties do not depend on the amount of the substance being described. Density, melting point, and malleability are examples of intensive properties. Extensive properties vary directly with the size of the object. Mass, electrical resistance, and number of moles of particles are all extensive properties.

Post-Lab Questions
1. Mass, volume, depth, and height are all extensive properties.
2. Color, density, phase, texture, and viscosity are intensive properties.
3. This can be demonstrated for either mass or volume. Students can show that 20 ml + 20 ml + 20 ml = 60 ml or 20 g + 20 g + 20 g = 60 g.
4. Intensive properties include color, temperature, texture, grain size, proportions of different minerals, and density. Extensive properties include mass, volume, and number of grains or crystals.

SC*LINKS*
THE WORLD'S A CLICK AWAY

Topic: Properties of Liquids
Go to: *www.scilinks.org*
Code: THC18

ACTIVITY 22: CREATING A COLLOID

Objective
Students will create a substance that does not clearly fall into the categories of solid, liquid, gas, or plasma.

Topic: Colloids
Go to: *www.scilinks.org*
Code: THC19

Purpose
Students will practice their skills of observation and analyzing discrepant events in experimenting with this colloid.

Materials
Shallow bowl, water, cornstarch

Notes
This is a demonstration that every student should see. They love to play with this colloid, it is completely nontoxic, and they like to share it with family. It is inexpensive, impressive, not dangerous, and fun.

Post-Lab Questions
1. It does not fit clearly into either category. It is actually a liquid with a solid suspended in it. Under certain conditions, it acts like a liquid. Under certain conditions, it acts like a solid.
2. Yes, because the slow pressure of the house and the addition of rain or rising water in the river could cause the house to sink and/or wash away
3. No, you cannot because they all dissolve in the water. To form a colloid, the solid must be suspended in the liquid, not dissolved in it.

ACTIVITY 23: AVERAGE ATOMIC MASS SIMULATION

Objective
Students will use a large number of small objects to find the average mass of the objects.

Purpose
Students will understand how an average mass is obtained and that it does not necessarily apply to every individual object.

Topic: Atomic Mass of Elements
Go to: *www.scilinks.org*
Code: THC20

Materials
100 small objects such as rice, dried beans, or popcorn kernels; homemade balance (Activity 2)

Notes
Even though the single-beam balance is not perfect, this lab does not require a perfect answer. The idea is for students to see that you can figure out the average mass by weighing a large sample and dividing by the sample number, and that the more samples there are, the more accurate the value will be.

Post-Lab Questions
1. Answers will vary, but the two averages were probably not the same.
2. No, it likely would not be the same, and if it happened to be, you could find the mass of another and it would not be.
3. The sample size of 100 is better because there are more of the item and therefore you will be more likely to get a representative sample. If you only pick 5 and they happen to be 5 of the biggest ones, then the average will come out high. The chance of choosing just the large ones and not the small ones shrinks as you choose a larger sample size.

ACTIVITY 24: REACTION RATE

Objective
Students will dissolve pieces of Alka-Seltzer tablets in water after crushing them and heating the water, and then time how long the reaction takes to complete.

Purpose
Students will see that smaller particle size and higher temperature both increase the reaction rate.

Materials
Alka-Seltzer or other effervescent tablet (The effervescent denture-cleaner tablets at 99-cent stores are pretty small, so students might need 2 of them.), water

Notes
Students should be aware that the tablets do not just dissolve; there is also a chemical reaction going on, as evidenced by the generation of bubbles. It is not critical that the masses of the pieces of tablet are identical. The difference in reaction rates is quite extreme, so a small difference in mass will not matter much.

Post-Lab Questions
1. 2 and 4
2. 3 and 4
3. Slower, faster, faster
4. Crush the chemicals into a powder, add the chemicals to warm water, encourage stirring

Topic: Reaction Rates
Go to: *www.scilinks.org*
Code: THC21

ACTIVITY 25: MOLECULAR MOTION AND TEMPERATURE

Objectives
Students will see how the rate of diffusion varies in cold, room temperature, and hot water.

Topic: Diffusion
Go to: *www.scilinks.org*
Code: THC22

Purpose
Students will see that the faster-moving molecules of hot water diffuse colors faster than slower-moving cold water because the molecules are vibrating more quickly. This will prepare them to understand kinetic molecular theory by giving them a real-world experience that can serve as a connection to the material.

Materials
3 cups or glasses, food coloring or colored drink

Notes
This is an effective yet simple lab. Students will be able to see clearly the difference in diffusion rates. In the follow-up to the lab, reinforce that the increased diffusion is because of the increased collisions from the faster-moving molecules. Because students cannot see the molecules, they cannot always make the connection automatically.

Post-Lab Questions
1. Hot, room temperature, cold
2. The hot water molecules were vibrating faster so they bumped the colors around faster.
3. In a rock concert where everyone is moving and bouncing around, you could end up far from your original location once the music starts playing. This is like the hot water. At a classical music concert, everyone sits in their seat and does not move very much. This is like the cold water.

ACTIVITY 26: BOILING WATER IN A SYRINGE

Objective
Students will make warm water boil by reducing the pressure inside a syringe.

Purpose
Students will see the effect of lowering the atmospheric pressure on the boiling point of a liquid. This will help them understand how vapor pressure and atmospheric pressure affect boiling point.

Materials
Hot water, coffee cup, syringe

Notes
Students will take warm water and cause it to boil by pulling out on the plunger of a syringe. If a student pulls 15–60 ml, they can lower the pressure to 0.25 atm or 25 kPa. Using a table of vapor pressures (see below), the teacher can point out how cool the water could be and still boil at this pressure (approximately 65°C). This goes well with the demonstration of boiling water in a bell jar connected to a vacuum pump, but this is much less expensive.

Post-Lab Questions
1. Pressure = 1(10/60) = 0.167 atm (101.3 kPa/1atm) = 17 kPa
2. Water vapor, not air
3. The hand boiler is already under low pressure. Because it is an alcohol with a low boiling point already, the warmth of your hand is enough to boil the liquid.

SCLINKS
THE WORLD'S A CLICK AWAY

Topic: Atmospheric Pressure
Go to: *www.scilinks.org*
Code: THC23

Extension

Vapor Pressures of Water

Temperature (°C)	Vapor pressure (kPa)	Vapor pressure (kPa)
0	0.6	4.5
3	0.8	6.0
5	0.9	6.8
8	1.1	8.3
10	1.2	9.0
12	1.4	10.5
14	1.6	12.0
16	1.8	13.5
18	2.1	15.8
19	2.2	16.5
20	2.3	17.3
21	2.5	18.8
22	2.6	19.5
23	2.8	21.0
24	3.0	22.5
25	3.2	24.0
26	3.4	25.5
27	3.6	27.0
28	3.8	28.5
29	4.0	30.0
30	4.2	31.5
32	4.8	36.0
35	5.6	42.0
40	7.4	55.5
50	12.3	92.3
60	19.9	149.3
70	31.2	234.1
80	47.3	354.9
90	70.1	525.9
100	101.3	760.0

ACTIVITY 27: LIFTING AN ICE CUBE WITH A STRING

Objective
Students will lift an ice cube by sprinkling salt over a string on the ice.

Purpose
Students will see that ice can be used to lower the freezing point of water temporarily.

Materials
Ice cube, cup, water, string, salt, sugar, other soluble substance

Notes
This does not always work the first time, so students should try it several times if it does not work. Salt lowers the freezing point of water, so the ice around the string begins to melt. Melting requires an input of energy, so it extracts some energy from the surrounding water and freezes it around and through the absorbent string. Then the cube can be lifted with the string.

Wrap-Up
An ice cube that comes out of the freezer is actually below the normal freezing point of the water (0°C). Depending on the settings in your freezer and how long the ice has been out of the freezer, it could be anywhere from –2°C to –10°C. Through a process called freezing point depression, a solute dissolved in a solvent lowers the freezing point of the solvent.

If the water's freezing point can be dropped to below its actual temperature, it will melt. In the process of melting, the ice will require energy input. When it takes this energy from the water around it, this can cause the water around it to freeze and hold on to the piece of string. The salt is necessary to lower the freezing point of the ice.

ACTIVITY 28: CHEMICAL FORMULA SIMULATIONS

Objective
Students will construct molecules out of papers they cut out to determine the chemical formula and the method for writing chemical formulas.

Purpose
Students will learn that chemical formulas can be written by exchanging the oxidation number of each ion.

Materials
Photocopy of Atom Cutouts page (p. 239), scissors

Notes
This activity is surprisingly effective for getting students to understand and remember how to write chemical formulas. Encourage students to keep the papers they cut out, as they will use them in another lab.

Problems
1. AC
2. A_2D
3. A_2F
4. A_3G
5. IB_2
6. ID
7. I_3G_2
8. UC_3
9. U_2F_3
10. UG
11. CH_4
12. $CaCl_2$
13. Na_2S
14. MgO
15. Be_3N_2

Topic: Chemical Formulas
Go to: *www.scilinks.org*
Code: THC24

ACTIVITY 29: CHEMICAL REACTION SIMULATION

Objective

Students will use their ion pieces to simulate the finishing and balancing of chemical equations.

Purpose

Students will understand how to figure out whether a chemical reaction is single displacement or double displacement, as well as how to determine the products of these reactions. Some students will already realize the equations need to be balanced, so the balanced answers are included and are also acceptable.

Materials

Atom Cutouts page (p. 239)

Notes

This is a surprisingly effective activity. If students have already done the chemical equation simulation lab, this one should be fairly easy. This method prevents the mistake of putting two anions or cations together. Once the activity is moved to real chemicals, students might have to be reminded not to put anions or cations together. It is valuable to come up with an analogy to explain how to tell whether or not a single displacement reaction will really happen using the activity series. It could be a beauty contest, an arm-wrestling match, or a square dance. Tell a funny story to go along with it and students will remember the activity for a long time and find it very useful.

Problems

1. $A + IF \rightarrow A_2F + I$ balanced would be $2A + IF \rightarrow A_2F + I$
2. $IC_2 + D \rightarrow ID + C$ balanced would be $IC_2 + D \rightarrow ID + 2C$

3. $O + U_2D_3 \rightarrow OD + U$ balanced would be $3O + U_2D_3 \rightarrow 3OD + 2U$
4. $UB_3 + G \rightarrow UG + B$ balanced would be $UB_3 + G \rightarrow UG + 3B$
5. $O + UG \rightarrow O_3G_2 + U$ balanced would be $3O + 2UG \rightarrow O_3G_2 + 2U$

Real Chemicals

6. $Mg + HCl \rightarrow MgCl_2 + H_2$ balanced would be $Mg + 2HCl \rightarrow MgCl_2 + H_2$
7. $Na_2S + I_2 \rightarrow NaI + S$ balanced would be $Na_2S + I_2 \rightarrow 2NaI + S$
8. $CaO + Br_2 \rightarrow CaBr_2 + O_2$ balanced would be $2CaO + 2Br_2 \rightarrow 2CaBr_2 + O_2$
9. $Al_2O_3 + Ba \rightarrow BaO + Al$ balanced would be $Al_2O_3 + 3Ba \rightarrow 3BaO + 2Al$

Problems

10. $E_2D + IC_2 \rightarrow EC + ID$ balanced would be $E_2D + IC_2 \rightarrow 2EC + ID$
11. $A_2D + IF \rightarrow A_2F + ID$ balanced would be $A_2D + IF \rightarrow A_2F + ID$
12. $OC_2 + E_2D \rightarrow OD + EC$ balanced would be $OC_2 + E_2D \rightarrow OD + 2EC$
13. $UG + EC \rightarrow UC_3 + E_3G$ balanced would be $UG + 3EC \rightarrow UC_3 + E_3G$
14. $OF + I_3G_2 \rightarrow O_3G_2 + IF$ balanced would be $3OF + I_3G_2 \rightarrow O_3G_2 + 3IF$

Real Chemicals

15. $NaCl + CaI_2 \rightarrow NaI + CaCl_2$ balanced would be $2NaCl + CaI_2 \rightarrow 2NaI + CaCl_2$
16. $KNO_3 + LiF \rightarrow KF + LiNO_3$ is already balanced
17. $H_2SO_4 + Li_2O \rightarrow H_2O + Li_2SO_4$ is already balanced
18. $Fe_2O_3 + NaOH \rightarrow Fe(OH)_3 + Na_2O$ balanced is $Fe_2O_3 + 6NaOH \rightarrow 2Fe(OH)_3 + 3Na_2O$
19. $CuSO_4 + HNO_3 \rightarrow Cu(NO_3)_2 + H_2SO_4$ balanced is $CuSO_4 + HNO_3 \rightarrow Cu(NO_3)_2 + H_2SO_4$

ACTIVITY 30: BALANCING CHEMICAL EQUATIONS SIMULATION

Objectives
Students will use paper cutouts to simulate chemical reactions and balancing products and reactants.

SC/LINKS.
THE WORLD'S A CLICK AWAY

Topic: Chemical Equations
Go to: *www.scilinks.org*
Code: THC26

Purpose
Students will see that only coefficients can be used to balance chemical equations and learn the logic behind balancing equations. Understanding the logic helps students greatly when they are learning the algorithms for balancing equations.

Students may need an extra copy of the atom cutout sheet to balance some of the equations. Two pages on which they can write should be included with the materials.

Materials
Atom Cutout page (p. 239), scissors

Notes
Students should be encouraged to build the molecules even if they think they know what they are doing. As they progress, they can try to do it without the molecules, but if they make the common balancing mistakes, then they should go back to building them.

Post-Lab Questions
1. $IC_2 + D \rightarrow ID + 2C$
2. $O + UD \rightarrow OD + U$
3. $UB_3 + G \rightarrow UG + 3B$
4. $A_2D + IF \rightarrow A_2F + ID$
5. $OC_2 + E_2D \rightarrow OD + 2EC$
6. $UG + 3EC \rightarrow UC_3 + E_3G$

Real Chemicals

7. $CaCl_2 + 2Na \rightarrow 2NaCl + Ca$
8. $2KF + O_2 \rightarrow K_2O + F_2$
9. $CuI_2 + 2LiBr \rightarrow CuBr_2 + 2LiI$
10. $MgO + 2HCl \rightarrow MgCl_2 + H_2O$
11. $2H_2 + O_2 \rightarrow 2H_2O$
12. $2Al + 3Cl2 \rightarrow 2AlCl_3$

ACTIVITY 31: MOLECULAR SHAPE

Objective
Students will determine whether the shape of a water molecule is linear or bent.

Purpose
Students will begin to understand VSEPR shapes and how the shape of a molecule affects its properties. They will also be introduced to the idea of polar and nonpolar molecules.

Materials
Comb, balloon, or other source of static electricity; water faucet

Notes
The weather can affect the success of this activity, but it works perfectly 99% of the time. During the follow-up to this activity in class, make sure that all students got the correct result that the stream of water bends.

Post-Lab Questions
1. The water stream bends toward the charged object.
2. The diagram showing the bent shape of the water molecule
3. Water is polar due to its bent shape.

SC*L*INKS.
THE WORLD'S A CLICK AWAY

Topic: Molecular Shapes
Go to: *www.scilinks.org*
Code: THC27

ACTIVITY 32: IDENTIFYING TYPES OF STREETLIGHTS LAB

Objective

Students will build an apparatus that will allow them to see the spectrum created by different streetlights.

Purpose

Students will learn that the spectrum given off by an excited gas can be used to identify the gas.

Materials

Shoe box, CD, scissors

Teacher Materials

Teachers should order the Night Spectra Quest Spectrum Card from Edmund Scientifics (approximately $5). The card can be used over and over. Students compare their results to this card (placed on the teacher's desk) to figure out what kind of streetlights they analyzed.

Notes

As more types of streetlights are made, some might be found that are not on this list. A slit is used in spectroscopes to provide distinct lines. Students need to make very thin slits in the spectroscope so that it will match the diagrams of the spectra on the cards. If the slit is too large, the colors may interfere with them.

Post-Lab Questions

1. Usually, the lights do not match perfectly. There can be moonlight, stray light, car headlights, or other lights that interfere with the match.

SC*LINKS.*
THE WORLD'S A CLICK AWAY

Topic: Visible Spectrum
Go to: *www.scilinks.org*
Code: THC28

2. There can be certain bright lines that are only in that type of light, or there can be certain colors that are in all of the lights except for that one to eliminate all of the others. There can also be distinct patterns only present in one type of light. So, it is only if the light being analyzed has a unique feature that it can be identified with certainty.

3. A slit is used to produce lines similar to the diagrams on the Night Spectra Quest card and so that the colors do not overlap each other.

ACTIVITY 33: GROWING CRYSTALS

Objective
Students will grow crystals of sugar, sodium chloride, and Epsom salts.

SCI*LINKS*
THE WORLD'S A CLICK AWAY

Topic: Crystalline Solids
Go to: *www.scilinks.org*
Code: THC29

Purpose
Students will see how to saturate and supersaturate a solution to form crystals.

Materials
Cups, water, sugar, salt, Epsom salt, thread

Notes
Most students have never grown crystals before and do not even know that rock candy is just big sugar crystals. They also do not realize that if you look at sugar, salt, or Epsom salt under a magnifying glass, you can see they are actually crystals. You may want to borrow a dissecting scope from a biology teacher or some magnifying glasses from the physics teacher to view the crystals first. Instruct students to try to remove any "crust" that forms on the surface of the liquid as it evaporates. If they push it down, most of the crystals will form on the bottom.

Post-Lab Questions
1. Answers will vary, but usually sugar crystals grow the largest.
2. Answers will vary but should be similar to cubes, cubes with pyramids on the ends, long spikes, etc.
3. In general, the crystals do not follow this pattern because of the number of variables involved. The density of each substance is different. The amount of water and sunlight, evaporation, and solute may vary. All of these variables will affect the size and rate of formation of the crystals.

ACTIVITY 34: DECOMPOSITION OF WATER LAB

Objective
Students will decompose water by running electricity through inert conductors.

Purpose
Students will see that twice as much hydrogen as oxygen is formed during the decomposition of water.

Materials
Glass, water, 9 V battery, wires or battery clip, pencil lead, pinch of salt

Notes
The graphite is necessary because it is inert. If you put the copper wire in the water, other reactions will happen and only one side will bubble and chlorine gas is produced. Discussions of anode and cathode were left out because books deal with the subject differently. To prevent confusion with your textbook or state standards, the discussion will be left to the teacher. It also is not pertinent to understanding this activity.

Post-Lab Questions
1. The black wire (or the wire coming from the negative terminal) bubbled faster because the hydrogen gas is produced there.
2. Oxygen was produced more slowly and hydrogen more quickly.
3. In a decomposition reaction, the balanced equation tells you how many moles of each product can be produced for each mole of reactant. In the decomposition of water, every two moles of water produce two moles of hydrogen and one mole of oxygen. Therefore the hydrogen is produced twice as fast as the oxygen.

SCiLINKS
THE WORLD'S A CLICK AWAY

Topic: Properties of Water
Go to: *www.scilinks.org*
Code: THC14

ACTIVITY 35: SOLUBILITY LAB

Objective
Students will judge the solubility of three solids and three liquids.

Purpose
Students will determine if different solids and liquids are polar or nonpolar by seeing if they dissolve in other substances.

Materials
6 cups, oil, water, rubbing alcohol, salt, sugar, baking soda

Notes
Somehow students get unanticipated results for some of the combinations. They will tell me that sugar and salt do not dissolve in water. I think they are either putting too much of the solute or not enough of the solvent, or are being impatient and not waiting long enough.

Post-Lab Questions
1. All three solids dissolve in water. You may want to discuss at this point the dissolving of sugar in water and that it does not form ions like the others.
2. Water and alcohol mix, but oil does not. So water and alcohol are polar.
3. Antifreeze: polar, Epsom salt: polar, car oil: nonpolar, animal fat: nonpolar, NutraSweet: polar, sand: nonpolar. Have students think about whether or not each of these dissolves in water to figure the answers.

SCI**LINKS**
THE WORLD'S A CLICK AWAY

Topic: Solubility
Go to: *www.scilinks.org*
Code: THC30

ACTIVITY 36: SEA ICE LAB

Objective

Students will learn whether or not ice formed on the surface of ice water is salty.

Purpose

Students will use the idea of freezing point depression to explain why sea ice is not salty.

Materials

Water, plastic cup, salt

Notes

It takes an understanding of freezing point depression to be able to answer the post-lab questions. Therefore, this activity should be done after a discussion of freezing point depression.

Students may be surprised to see that the ice is not very salty. There may be some pockets of salt in bubbles in the ice, but otherwise, it is very fresh water. The more seasons that sea ice goes through, the less salty it gets.

Post-Lab Questions

1. The ice has the lowest salinity and the leftover water the highest.
2. 37 g NaCl in 1000 g solution
    37/58 = .64 mol NaCl, which is 1.28 moles sodium and chloride ions
    1.28 mol/1.0 kg = 1.28 molal
    $\Delta T = k_f m = 1.86°C/molal(1.28 \text{ molal}) = 2.38°C$ so the freezing point of ocean water is −2.38°C due to the salt.
3. Because of freezing point depression, the higher the concentration of salt, the lower the freezing point of the water. As the temperature drops, regions with the lowest concentration freeze first. If this process is stopped before the freezing is complete, the least salty water will be frozen and the most salty will not.

ACTIVITY 37: INVISIBLE INK LAB

Objective
Students will create an "invisible ink" and then test to see which chemical may be responsible for making it invisible.

Purpose
Students will begin to observe evidence of chemical reactions and practice testing one variable at a time.

Materials
Students determine what materials to use.

Notes
This is set up as an inquiry activity in that students are shown how to develop the invisible ink, and then the rest of the procedure is up to them. If you wish to give more instruction—such as specific chemicals to test and how to test them—feel free. But by now, students should be comfortable with some freedom in the procedure and data collection.

Post-Lab Questions
1. Organic liquids will work well. Anything with sugar or organic acids will work. Diet soft drinks likely will not work. Chemicals such as ammonia will not work well. The organic chemicals will turn brown when heated. Some other chemicals will make the paper puff up, but that should not be considered invisible ink.
2. Answers will vary depending on what they consider success. For the browning reaction, usually sugar or organic acids are required.
3. Example: "Because Diet Coke didn't work and Diet Sprite did, I figured that it is something in the lemon juice. So, I tried lemon juice and it worked. So, I dissolved a vitamin C tablet in water and it didn't work, so it's not vitamin C. I then dissolved sugar in water and it did work. So, sugar is definitely involved in the reaction."

SC**LINKS**.
THE WORLD'S A CLICK AWAY

Topic: Chemical Reactions
Go to: *www.scilinks.org*
Code: THC25

ACTIVITY 9: SOLUTIONS, SUSPENSIONS, AND MIXTURES

QUESTION ?

Can the components of solutions, suspensions, and mixtures be separated with a filter?

SAFETY

Because you will test some chemicals of your choice in this activity, you should wear goggles since the chemicals have unknown dangers. Discard all materials upon finishing. Do not eat or drink any of the products after the experiment.

MATERIALS

Salt or sugar, coffee filter, baby powder or cornstarch, sand or dirt, water, food coloring, baking soda, other food ingredients (for mixing)

PROCEDURE

Some chemicals dissolve in water to make a solution; some do not dissolve but remain suspended in the water, making a suspension; and some do not dissolve and sink right to the bottom, making a mixture. It is important in chemistry to understand which of these chemicals can be filtered out. In this activity, you will make one of each and pass them through a coffee filter.

1. Make a solution of sugar or salt and pour it through a coffee filter. Does it filter out?
2. Make a suspension of a very small amount of baby powder or cornstarch (a spoonful of powder or starch in a small cup of water). Does it filter out?
3. Make a mixture of sand or dirt and water. Does it filter out?
4. Try several other combinations on your own (food coloring, baking soda, etc.). Do they filter out? Do not select anything harmful; use only food ingredients.

Post-Lab Questions

1. Can a solution be filtered? Can a suspension be filtered? Can a mixture be filtered?
2. Soda passes right through a filter paper. Is it a solution, suspension, or mixture? Pulp can be filtered from orange juice and sinks to the bottom of a cup. Is it a solution, suspension, or mixture?
3. Some people think there is plenty of freshwater on Earth because we can just filter the salt from salt water in the oceans. Is this true? Explain.

Extension

Another way to tell the difference between a solution and a suspension is to shine a flashlight or laser through the mixture. If the beam is visible, then it is bouncing off the particles in a suspension. If it is not visible, then it is passing right through a solution. Try this method to test the three combinations that you passed through a filter. Do your results agree?

ACTIVITY 10: SEPARATION LAB: ELEMENTS, COMPOUNDS, AND MIXTURES

QUESTION ❓

Can a sample of salt, sand, Styrofoam, and iron be separated using only their physical properties?

SAFETY

If you need to evaporate something, do not heat it; leave it on a windowsill to dry. Because of the possibility of getting abrasive chemicals in the eye, wear goggles during this activity. Keep all materials out of the reach of children.

MATERIALS

Bag of mixture, an assortment of separating tools that will vary by student

PROCEDURE

Pre-Lab Questions
1. Name 3 physical properties for each of the substances.
2. Name 2 chemical properties for each of the substances.

In this lab, you will determine whether the combination of salt, sand, iron, and Styrofoam results in a compound or a mixture. If you are able to separate the components without any chemical reactions, then it is a mixture. If you cannot separate them physically, then it is a compound. You will be given the premeasured mixture and have the task of separating the four components if you can.

The procedure will be entirely up to you, but you need to record each step in your lab report. Once you have separated each component, you should wrap the container in plastic wrap and turn it in to have its mass checked. Plan ahead!

Post-Lab Questions

1. Which property of each substance did you use to separate it from the rest?
2. Was this a compound or a mixture?
3. Name 3 compounds and 3 mixtures.

ACTIVITY 11: PROBABILITY OF FINDING AN ELECTRON

QUESTION ❓

What does it mean to say that an electron has a probability of being found in a certain location around the nucleus?

SAFETY 🩹

No safety concerns. Return all materials to the box, put the lid on, and keep the box out of the reach of young children.

MATERIALS 📏

Pen or pencil, copy of target (p. 235)

PROCEDURE ✏️

It is known that electrons do not actually fly around in fixed orbits like planets. When you see textbook drawings of electrons in orbits, the orbits only represent where it is the most probable that the electron may be found at any moment. Sometimes this is called the electron cloud. The electrons also do not form a cloud; that is just a model representing the likelihood that an electron will be found at a certain location. You will simulate this probability analysis by dropping a pen at a target and counting how many times the pen marks in each area.

1. Take the target paper and put it on the floor. Holding the pen at arm's length, drop it 50 times, tip first, so that it will make a mark on the paper.
2. Count how many times the pen struck each of the areas on the target. If it is on the line, try to determine which side it is closer to hitting. Then count the total hits inside of that circle (e.g., for circle 4, that would be all the hits in circles 1, 2, 3, and 4).
3. Fill in the chart and then graph your results with a smooth curve. Then calculate the probability using the equation (total hits/total drops) × 100.

Data

Circle 1	Hits =	Total hits =	Area = 4.9 cm²	Probability = _____ %
Circle 2	Hits =	Total hits =	Area = 14.7 cm²	Probability = _____ %
Circle 3	Hits =	Total hits =	Area = 24.5 cm²	Probability = _____ %
Circle 4	Hits =	Total hits =	Area = 34.4 cm²	Probability = _____ %
Circle 5	Hits =	Total hits =	Area = 44.2 cm²	Probability = _____ %
Circle 6	Hits =	Total hits =	Area = 53.0 cm²	Probability = _____ %

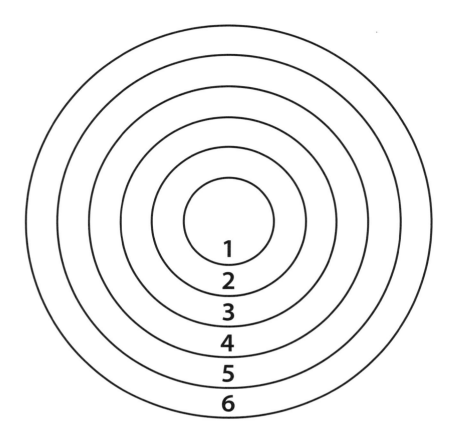

Note: Do not use the above diagram to do this activity. You will be given a full-size diagram to use for the experiment

Post-Lab Questions
1. In which circle did the most hits occur?
2. Scientists consider the size of the 1s orbital to be the circle in which there is a 90% chance of finding the 1s electron. Which is the smallest circle that contains 90% of your dots (45 dots)?
3. If you dropped your pen one more time, could you assume that it will fall in the ring noted in #1?

ACTIVITY 12: HALF-LIFE SIMULATION

QUESTION

What is the half-life of a simulated nuclear reaction?

SAFETY

Be careful with the scissors and keep them out of the reach of small children.

MATERIALS

Copy of provided paper (p. 237), scissors, box

PROCEDURE

In this lab, you will simulate the graphing of the half-life of a radioactive substance using slips of paper. A half-life is defined as the time that it takes for half of a radioactive material to decay into another substance. You will simulate this process by flipping some papers and taking out all that are facing the same direction and continuing. The papers with the symbol facing down represent atoms that are radioactive. Those facing up have already decayed.

Cut out all the pieces of paper with the Greek letter α on them. Put them in a box and shake them up. Take out all the pieces that have the α facing up. Count and record how many are left. Shake the box again, and again remove all of the pieces that have the α facing up. Count and record how many are left. Continue this until no pieces are left. Repeat this procedure one more time.

Data

Trial Number	Number of Papers Left
1	100
2	
3	
4	
5	
6	
7	

α	α	α	α	α	α	α	α	α	α
α	α	α	α	α	α	α	α	α	α
α	α	α	α	α	α	α	α	α	α
α	α	α	α	α	α	α	α	α	α
α	α	α	α	α	α	α	α	α	α
α	α	α	α	α	α	α	α	α	α
α	α	α	α	α	α	α	α	α	α
α	α	α	α	α	α	α	α	α	α
α	α	α	α	α	α	α	α	α	α
α	α	α	α	α	α	α	α	α	α

Note: Do not use the alpha pieces on this page. You will be given a full-size copy to cut out and use for this activity.

Prepare a graph with trial # on the *x*-axis and the number of papers left on the *y*-axis.

Papers Left

Trial #

Post-Lab Questions

1. How many shakes did it take to get rid of all the papers?
2. Use your graph to interpolate the half-life if each shake represents 1,000 years. Use a ruler and be as accurate as possible. Report your answer in years.
3. Use your graph to answer the question, "How many years have passed when 25% of the papers are left?"
4. According to your data, what is the oldest object that this method could be used to date?

ACTIVITY 13: RUTHERFORD'S GOLD FOIL SIMULATION

QUESTION ❓

How can simple probabilities be used to indirectly measure the diameter of a marble?

SAFETY

Marbles are a choking hazard for small children and a slip-and-fall hazard if left lying around. Pack up all the materials, replace the lid, and put the box out of the reach of children. Be sure to move all fragile items out of the area to avoid breaking glass or ceramic objects.

MATERIALS

Ruler, 6 marbles

PROCEDURE

In this lab, you will simulate the famous experiment by Ernest Rutherford. In this experiment, Rutherford shot particles at a very thin sheet of gold foil. Behind the gold foil was a screen that would light up when a particle hit it. He noticed that most of the particles went straight through the foil and only a small percentage was deflected. He concluded that the nucleus of those gold atoms makes up only a very small part of the atom's volume. From this observation came the phrase, "Atoms are mostly empty space." You will simulate this experiment with marbles. By rolling a marble at 5 targets and counting how many times you hit, you will be able to calculate the diameter of a marble accurately. Do not let the math scare you; this involves nothing more difficult than multiplying or dividing.

Set up a track to keep the marbles inside by placing 2 books 50 cm apart (see below). Place the 5 target marbles within that 50 cm, not worrying if they are perfectly spaced. It is very important that you do not aim at the marbles, but just roll them randomly. There are a few ways you can ensure randomness: You can turn around and roll the marble backward, stand far away from the targets, or kick the marble. Record how many times you hit the target marbles out of 100 rolls.

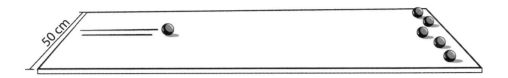

Answers to Frequently Asked Questions

1. If the marble hits one marble, bounces off it, and hits another one, does that count as two hits?
   No, only one hit is allowed per roll.
2. If the marble hits the wall behind the marbles and bounces back and hits a marble, does it count?
   No, it must hit as it passes the marbles the first time.
3. After a marble gets hit, do I put it back in line?
   Yes, put it back so that no marble blocks the path to another marble.
4. If the rolled marble hits the book, does it count?
   No, that roll was not within the 50 cm track. Do it over.
5. I missed the first 10 shots. Am I doing something wrong?
   No, the marbles take up a small percentage of the track, so you will hit them a small percentage of the time. If each marble were 2 cm (which they are not), you would only hit 40% of the time, or 40 out of 100 times. Marbles are smaller than that, so you will hit less often than that.

Data

Number of tries _____

Number of hits _____

Calculations

1. First, figure out the ratio of times that you hit to times that you tried: hits/tries. Do not leave it in fraction format; convert it to a decimal with your calculator.
2. Because you are rolling one marble at another, if they are within two diameters of each other, they will collide, so they appear to be taking up twice as much space as they really do. So divide your answer to #1 by 2. This is the proportion of the track that the marbles occupy.

3. Now multiply your answer from #2 by the width of the track to determine how much of the track's space the marbles take up.
4. Now divide by 5, the number of target marbles, to figure out how much space each marble took up. This is the diameter of the marble.

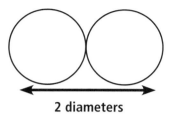

2 diameters

Post-Lab Questions

1. Ask your teacher to measure a marble using a caliper, micrometer, or other accurate measuring device. What was the percent difference between your answer and this directly measured answer?
2. Why was it important for you to not aim at the marbles?
3. Why did you have to roll the marble so many times? What could have happened if you only rolled it 3 or 4 times?

Extension

Collect all the data from students in all of the chemistry classes at school and do the calculation again. Theoretically, the more numbers you get, the more accurate your answer will be. If you have taken statistics, you can calculate a Q test to see whether some of the very high and very low data can be thrown out.

Activity adapted from Robinson, P., and P. G. Hewitt. 1987. *Conceptual physics laboratory manual.* 8th ed. Menlo Park, CA: Addison-Wesley.

ACTIVITY 14:
MEAN FREE PATH
ACTIVITY

QUESTION ?

What is the average distance between atoms (also known as mean free path)?

MATERIALS

Ruler, target diagram

PROCEDURE

Mean free path is the average distance an atom has to move before colliding with another atom. This is approximately the distance between molecules or atoms. It is usually used when dealing with gases and plasmas. Mean free path is important for understanding temperature and pressure and in nuclear chemistry, optics, and sound propagation. Mean free path is important when analyzing chemical reactions that involve gases, calculating the conductivity or density of a gas, and working with plasmas such as in a fluorescent lightbulb or in a fusion reactor. (See the Wikipedia entry for more details about the applications of mean free path.) Remember that the word *mean* used in this context means the same thing as *average*.

Consider the diagram on page 118 in which there are many circles representing atoms or molecules of a gas or plasma in a container. Measure the distances between 10 of the atoms and their closest neighbors. Take the average of those 10 distances to find the mean free path. Be sure to use centimeters when measuring. One distance has already been marked for you.

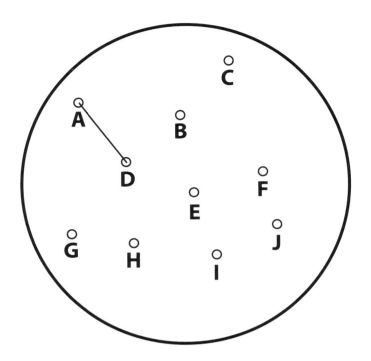

Data

Number	1st Atom	2nd Atom	Distance (cm)
1	A	D	
2			
3			
4			
5			
6			
7			
8			
9			
10			
Mean			

Post-Lab Questions

1. If two of these atoms were very close together, would it have changed your answer very much? Explain.
2. If you were to increase the number of atoms or molecules in this container, how would it change the mean free path? Explain.
3. If you were to increase the size of the container, how would it change the mean free path? Explain.

ACTIVITY 15: FREEZING WATER

QUESTION ?

When ice melts, is the volume of water less than or greater than the volume of the ice?

SAFETY

Use only clean water for this activity. Do not work near electrical appliances or outlets. Clean up any spills immediately.

MATERIALS

Syringe, syringe cap, ice cube, water, pencil

PROCEDURE

In this lab, you will determining which is bigger, an ice cube or the water that results when the ice cube melts. You will do this by measuring the volume of a piece of ice, then letting the ice melt and measuring the volume of the water.

Get an ice cube that will fit inside your syringe. Cap the syringe and put 25 ml of water in it. Get all of the air bubbles out and check your measurement again. Put the ice cube in and push it down with a pencil or another thin object. Do not let the pencil go underwater, but make sure that the entire ice cube is under. Record the volume. Now let the ice cube melt and record the volume again.

Data

1. Volume of water _____ ml
2. Volume of ice and water _____ ml
3. Volume of ice _____ ml
4. Volume of melted ice and water _____ ml
5. Difference between #2 and #4 _____ ml

Post-Lab Questions

1. Was the water level higher before or after the ice melted?
2. Does this mean water expands or contracts when it freezes?
3. How does this explain why you should not put sealed containers (such as soda cans) in the freezer?
4. Assuming that the mass of the ice and water does not change during this experiment, which is more dense, ice or water? Support your answer with observations from your personal experiences.

ACTIVITY 16:
SURFACE TENSION LAB

QUESTION ?

How strong is the surface tension of water?

SAFETY

Do not leave pennies where a child might swallow them. Use only clean water in the syringe. Press the plunger of the syringe gently. Clean up all spills immediately. Do not work near electrical appliances or outlets.

MATERIALS

Penny, water, syringe, dishwashing liquid

PROCEDURE

In this lab, you will test surface tension by counting how many drops of water you can put on a penny before it overflows. Dishwashing liquid breaks up surface tension, so you will repeat the experiment again after putting a little dishwashing liquid in the water. Surface tension is a simple way to estimate the intermolecular forces in a substance. Intermolecular forces are attractions between molecules or atoms that hold the particles together. Intermolecular forces affect properties such as boiling point and surface tension.

First, predict how many drops of water you think you will be able to put on the penny. Lay a penny on a flat surface with the tails side facing up. Using your syringe, carefully count the number of drops you place on the penny until the water overflows. Clean and dry the penny. Now add a couple drops of dishwashing liquid to the water and repeat. When you have finished, clean the syringe until all of the dishwashing liquid is gone.

Data

Predicted number of drops _____ drops

Drops of tap water _____ drops

Drops of soapy water _____ drops

Post-Lab Questions

1. Did pure water or soapy water enable you to put more drops of water on the penny? Why?
2. If there was a chemical that could increase surface tension, do you think it would allow more drops or fewer drops?
3. Were you able to put more or fewer drops than you predicted?

ACTIVITY 17: DENSITY OF OIL LAB

QUESTION ❓

What is the density of cooking oil?

SAFETY

Clean everything very well with dishwashing liquid after this experiment to prevent the growth of mold. Do not use the oil for cooking when you have finished. Use only clean water. Squeeze the plunger on the syringe gently. Do not work near an electrical appliance or outlet. Clean up any spills immediately.

MATERIALS

Cooking oil, dishwashing liquid, water, syringe, balance (Activity 2)

PROCEDURE

In this lab, you will determine the density of oil by comparing it to water. We know that the density of water is 1.0 g/ml, and we will use this to calculate the density of the oil.

Set up your balance with one cup on each side. Put 30 ml of water in one of the cups. Now fill your syringe with cooking oil. Carefully add the oil to the other side of the balance until they are balanced and record how much oil was required to achieve the balance. Note that at this point the mass of water and the mass of oil are equal even though the volumes are not. Clean the syringe and the cup with dishwashing liquid to get the oil out.

Data

Volume of water <u>30 ml</u>

Volume of oil _____ ml

Calculations

1. What was the mass of the water used?
2. What was the mass of the oil needed to balance the water?
3. Use the mass and volume of the oil to calculate its density.

Post-Lab Questions

1. Which is denser, oil or water?
2. If you have equal masses of oil and water, which one will have the larger volume?
3. If you have equal volumes of oil and water, which one will have the larger mass?

Extension

Use a similar method to calculate the density of other objects, such as marbles, rocks, rubber balls, and so on. If any of the objects that you choose could be harmful to the eyes, be sure to wear goggles.

ACTIVITY 18: CHROMATOGRAPHY LAB

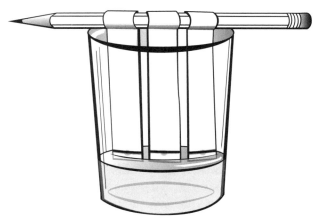

QUESTION ⁉

Are all colored inks made of the same components?

SAFETY 🩹

Use caution when working with scissors and keep them out of the reach of children.

MATERIALS 📏

Coffee filter, drinking glasses, pencils, scissors

PROCEDURE 👣

Chromatography is a very important technique in chemistry. There are many types of chromatography, including gas chromatography, thin film chromatography, high-performance liquid chromatography, and paper chromatography. These methods are used in quality assurance, forensic science, pharmacology, toxicology, agriculture, and almost every other area of chemistry. You will perform paper chromatography to identify the colors used to make black ink. It may seem strange that black ink is made up of colors, but inks are called subtractive colors. Each color subtracts part of the spectrum, leaving black when all of the colors of the spectrum are gone. There are different combinations that can create black this way, and different companies use different mixtures of subtractive colors.

Paper chromatography works by putting a sample on an absorbent paper and the paper draws the solvent slowly up the paper. Because some parts of the sample (the ink, in this case) are more soluble in the solvent than others and some attach to the paper more strongly than others, the samples will rise through the paper at different rates. Measuring an unknown sample's retention factor and then comparing it to known samples can make a match.

You will use paper chromatography to solve a simulated crime. Your teacher has a chromatograph run on a piece of evidence from a kidnapping ransom note. You have samples from three suspects' markers. You will attempt to make a match between one of your samples and the evidence.

You will make three chromatography papers from your coffee filter, each 2 in. long. Each one should have a mark at the bottom. Your teacher will help you make these papers in class.

1. Prepare a cup with a small amount of water in the bottom. Make sure the water is not deeper than the mark on the paper.
2. Hang the paper from a pencil using a piece of tape. Place the pencil across the top of the cup but do not let the water touch the mark. Leave the paper until the water line reaches the top.
3. Draw a diagram similar to the one below in your lab notebook. Attach your actual chromatograms next to them after they have dried. In the boxes that you draw in notebook, sketch the chromatograms by putting a line at the center of each colored section and measure the distance from the bottom of the paper to the line. Do the same for the evidence and give the colors of each section.
4. Compare your diagrams to the evidence that your teacher supplies.
5. For each of the colored lines, calculate the retention factor (r_f) using this formula:

$$r_f = \frac{\text{distance traveled by colored line}}{\text{distance traveled by liquid}}$$

Data

Sample A	Sample B	Sample C	Evidence

Post-Lab Questions

1. If this was a real crime scene investigation, could this method alone be used to absolutely identify the person who committed the crime? Explain.

2. Were any two of your samples similar to or the same as each other? Which ones?

3. Did you have two lines of the same color in different samples that had different retention rates? (In other words, did you have two blue lines that ended up in different places?)

ACTIVITY 19: DENSITY COLUMN IN A STRAW

QUESTION ❓

How do the densities of different sugar solutions compare to one another?

SAFETY

Discard the sugar solutions upon completion and do not drink the liquid. Wipe up any spills immediately.

MATERIALS

Sugar, water, transparent drinking straw, three small cups, food coloring or colored drinks (such as Kool-Aid or Gatorade)

PROCEDURE

Substances with different densities can be made to float on each other like water and oil. This also happens in the ocean as a result of different temperatures (thermoclines) or different salt concentrations (haloclines). Even though it is all salt water, liquids with different temperatures or concentrations can form layers even though it is the same liquid. You will simulate this effect using different solutions of sugar water.

1. Make three different solutions in small cups. The first cup is 30 ml of pure water, the second is 30 ml of water with a large spoonful of sugar, and the third is 30 ml of water with two large spoonfuls of sugar. Stir the solutions completely.
2. Put a drop of food coloring or colored drink in the middle cup so that you will be able to see the layers.
3. Dip the straw in the pure water and put your thumb over the end of the straw to keep it in. Now put the straw in the middle cup and release your thumb for a moment until the water rises, then put your thumb back over the straw. Now do it again with the third liquid. You could make stronger and stronger solutions and continue this until the straw is full.

Post-Lab Questions

1. In a thermocline, do you think that the warmer water or the colder water will be on top? Explain.
2. When a freshwater river flows into the ocean, will the freshwater stay on top of the salt water or go below? Explain.
3. Which is more dense, cooking oil or water? Explain how you could design a simple experiment to figure it out if you did not know.

ACTIVITY 20: MECHANOLUMINESCENCE: MAKING THINGS LIGHT UP

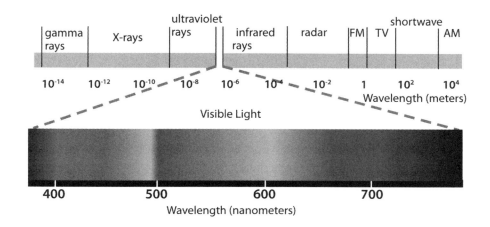

QUESTION ❓

Why does a Life Saver light up when crushed?

SAFETY

Be sure to look around before turning the lights off to notice any hazards. Be very careful biting down hard on candy, especially if you have had dental work done.

MATERIALS

Several Wint-O-Green Life Savers, transparent tape, 2 sugar cubes

PROCEDURE

Mechanoluminescence basically means making something light up with the use of force. There are many substances around you that are mechanoluminescent (also called triboluminescent or fractoluminescent). You will experience two substances and have the chance to try some on your own.

Wintergreen (methyl salicylate) cannot luminesce (give off light) through a force, but it can luminesce when ultraviolet light shines on it. The combination of the sugar and the wintergreen creates this effect. The sugar gives off some ultraviolet light when it is crushed, and the wintergreen absorbs the light and gives it off again in a color that our eyes can see. The energy the sugar gives off is mostly at about 350 nanometers (nm). Our eyes cannot see that light, in the same way our ears cannot hear a dog whistle. The wintergreen absorbs that energy and re-emits it at about 450 nm, which we can see. (See also *http://pages.towson.edu/ladon/wg/candywww. htm* for more information. If the link changes, search the internet for "Wintergreen Candy and Other Triboluminescent Materials" by Linda Sweeting.)

1. Have the two packs of Wint-O-Green Life Savers opened and the transparent tape roll ready so that you can find the end in the dark.
2. Go to a room with no windows. A bathroom works best. It must get very dark in this room and there must be a mirror. Let your eyes adjust to the darkness for 3–5 min.
3. Put the Life Saver standing up between your upper and lower teeth. Look into the mirror and bite down hard with your lips open. Keep chewing and record what you see. Repeat with the second candy.
4. Grab the end of the transparent tape and quickly pull about 12 in. (30 cm) off the roll. Record your observations.

Post-Lab Questions
1. What color did you see the candy luminesce?
2. What color did you see the transparent tape luminesce?
3. Find a picture of the electromagnetic spectrum either online or in your book and answer the following questions:

   a. What color should 450 nm be? Did that match your answer to #1?
   b. What do you think is the wavelength of the light given off by the transparent tape? Do you think that sugar or wintergreen had anything to do with this?
   c. If you can see any color at all from the sugar, what color do you think it would be?

Extension
If you have sugar cubes around the house, scrape two of them together quickly in the dark and observe. Try other candies such as Tic Tacs, Necco Wafers, or Pep-O-Mint Life Savers.

ACTIVITY 21: INTENSIVE AND EXTENSIVE PROPERTIES

QUESTION ❓

How do properties change as a solution is created?

SAFETY

Wipe up any spills immediately. Keep the lid on the box and keep the box out of the reach of children.

MATERIALS

3 small cups, food coloring or colored drinks

PROCEDURE

Intensive properties do not depend on the size of a sample. For example, because the texture of a sample does not depend on how big it is, texture is an intensive property. Extensive properties depend on the size of the sample. The weight or mass of an object depends on how much of the substance you have, so mass is an extensive property. In this lab, you will take a simple substance and perform some simple actions to shed light on intensive and extensive properties.

1. In a large cup, put some water and a couple of drops of food coloring and stir.
2. Write down five properties of this mixture (solution). If the property is a measurable property (such as temperature or volume), you can estimate if a measuring device is not available.
3. Now pour that liquid solution into three smaller cups. Write down five properties of the smaller cups.

Post-Lab Questions
1. Name three properties that changed when you poured the water into smaller cups. Are these intensive or extensive properties?
2. Name three properties that did not change during this activity. Are these intensive or extensive properties?
3. Choose an extensive property. When the liquid is split into three cups, does that property in the little cups add up to the property in the big cup?
4. Name three intensive properties and two extensive properties of a rock.

ACTIVITY 22: CREATING A COLLOID

QUESTION

What state of matter is a colloid?

SAFETY

Do not try to save the cornstarch and reuse it. Mold grows quickly on cornstarch once it is wet, so dispose of it immediately. Wipe up any spills immediately. Do not consume the cornstarch after use. Dispose of the material in the trash.

MATERIALS

Shallow bowl, water, cornstarch

PROCEDURE

The kinetic molecular theory helps one understand the difference between solid, liquid, gas, and plasma. A solid has a definite shape and volume. A liquid has a definite volume and takes the shape of its container. A gas fills its container completely and its volume changes with temperature and pressure. A plasma fills its container and has a variable volume.

In this lab, you will investigate a material called a colloid to determine its state of matter. You will see that determining the state of matter is not always as easy as it sounds. Colloids are not a separate state of matter, but they sure can act strangely.

1. Make the cornstarch colloid by adding 4 spoonfuls of cornstarch to 2 spoonfuls of water. It should be very thick but not dry. Make small adjustments by adding a little more starch or a little more water. It will dry out a little over time; just add more water to get the colloid back to its

original condition. The colloid should get to the point where you can pick up a chunk of it and it turns into a liquid in your hand.

2. After each of the following tests, determine whether the colloid acted like a liquid or a solid:

   a. Tap the surface of the colloid quickly with your finger. Is it a solid or a liquid? _____
   b. Press your finger slowly into the colloid. (It will not hurt you; it actually makes your skin soft and will rinse off with water.) Is it a solid or a liquid? _____
   c. Try to stir the colloid quickly with your finger. Is it a solid or a liquid? _____
   d. Try to stir the colloid slowly with your finger. Is it a solid or a liquid? _____
   e. Tip the bowl from side to side. Is it a solid or a liquid? _____
   f. Grab a chunk and pick it up. Is it a solid or a liquid? _____
   g. Pour it from the bowl to your hand. Is it a solid or a liquid? _____
   h. Set objects of different densities on its surface. Is it a solid or a liquid? _____

Post-Lab Questions

1. Is this colloid a solid or a liquid? Explain.
2. Many fine powders, such as the silt on the side of a river, can form colloids. Would it be dangerous to build homes or businesses on these riverbeds? Try a little experiment with your colloid to see what might happen.
3. Do you think you could make a colloid from salt, sugar, or baking soda? Based on your answer, what is one condition that must be met for a powder to form a colloid?

Extension

Take a field trip to an elementary school and share this activity with the students. Bring several examples of solids, liquids, and gases. Let them play with a "plasma globe" to experience the fourth state of matter. Check your state's science content standards to see at which grade level these subjects are taught.

ACTIVITY 23: AVERAGE ATOMIC MASS SIMULATION

QUESTION

How is the average atomic mass of an element calculated?

SAFETY

Dispose of the rice or beans when finished with this lab. Do not eat them. Use only clean water in your syringe. Clean up any spills immediately. Do not work near electrical appliances or outlets.

MATERIALS

100 small objects such as rice, dried beans, or popcorn kernels; homemade balance

PROCEDURE

Single atoms are much too small to weigh individually. To combat this, scientists can weigh large numbers of atoms at a time and then divide the weight by the number of atoms to find the average mass of a single atom. You may think all atoms of a certain element are the same, but they are not. For example, there are helium atoms that have two protons and one neutron (helium-3 mass = 3 amu) and two protons and two neutrons (helium-4 mass = 4 amu). So when the mass of helium is reported on the periodic table as 4.00260, it is the average of all the isotopes of helium. (Because electrons are so incredibly light compared to protons and neutrons, they are not even included in the calculation of atomic mass.) If you were actually able to hold one helium atom in your hand, it could not have a mass of 4.00260. But if you held a lot of helium atoms, they would have an average mass of 4.00260. In this lab, you will try to determine the average mass of a grain of rice in the same way.

1. Count out 50 grains of rice and find their mass using your balance. Record your result. If you do not have rice, you can use dried beans or popcorn kernels.
2. Add another 50 grains of rice and find their mass on your balance. Record your result.
3. Calculate the average mass of the rice and record your results.

Data

Mass of 50 grains of rice _____ g   Average mass of 1 grain _____ g

Mass of 100 grains of rice _____ g   Average mass of 1 grain _____ g

Post-Lab Questions

1. Were your two average masses exactly the same? Explain.
2. If you could find the mass of a single grain, do you think it would equal either of your averages?
3. Which of your averages do you think is the more accurate answer, if you had to choose one? Explain.

ACTIVITY 24: REACTION RATE

QUESTION ?

What affects the speed at which a chemical reaction occurs (reaction rate)?

SAFETY

Hot water should come from the tap, not from the microwave or stove. Use caution even with hot tap water. Goggles should be worn. Clean up any spills immediately.

MATERIALS

Alka-Seltzer or other effervescent tablet (The effervescent denture-cleaner tablets at 99-cent stores are pretty small, so students might need 2 of them.), water

PROCEDURE

There are several factors that affect the speed of a chemical reaction or reaction rate. In this lab, you will use Alka-Seltzer tablets to start a chemical reaction and then take several steps to adjust the reaction rate. Alka-Seltzer tablets have several acids (citric, ascorbic, etc.) and a base (sodium bicarbonate) in them. When they are dissolved in water, these chemicals react and make carbon dioxide bubbles as well as several other products. You will time how long it takes for a piece of the Alka-Seltzer tablet to completely react to determine the reaction rate.

Cut your Alka-Seltzer tablet into four pieces. If it breaks apart a little, that's OK; just keep the smaller pieces together. You will need to have four cups of water ready, two room temperature and two hot (not boiling, but hot water from the tap). In the first cup of cold water, add one piece of Alka-Seltzer tablet whole and time how long it takes to react completely. Next, crush up a tablet and add it to the second cup with cold water. For the third cup, add the intact piece of tablet to the hot water. For the last cup, crush the tablet and add it to the hot water.

Data

Create your own data chart to record how long it took for each sample to react completely, as well as any other observations that you made.

Post-Lab Questions

1. Which reacted faster, cup 1 or cup 2? Cup 3 or cup 4?
2. Which reacted faster, cup 1 or cup 3? Cup 2 or cup 4?
3. How do each of the following factors change reaction rate (i.e., make it faster or slower): cold water, hot water, crushing the tablet?
4. A company that makes flavored water is having trouble getting all of the natural flavorings to dissolve quickly. What would you recommend they do to make the process faster? Explain.

Extension

If you have another tablet, try the same experiment with cold water. Devise a method for testing the vinegar and baking soda reaction with cold and hot water. Does the same pattern apply to dissolving salt or sugar in hot and cold water?

ACTIVITY 25: MOLECULAR MOTION AND TEMPERATURE

QUESTION ❓

How does the temperature of water molecules affect their motion?

SAFETY

Be careful when using hot water. Clean up all spills immediately. Do not consume any of the liquids used, and do not use the cups as drinking cups.

MATERIALS

3 cups or glasses, food coloring or colored drink

PROCEDURE

In this lab, you will investigate how molecular motion is influenced by temperature. All molecules are in motion. The molecules vibrate, bouncing off each other and the walls of the container. When two different molecules are placed close together, they bounce off each other as well. If one molecule is visible, then how quickly it disperses should be a measure of how quickly the molecules are moving. When you spray perfume in a room with still air, it disperses through the room partly because of these random collisions.

1. Prepare three transparent cups or glasses of water approximately the same size with approximately the same amount of water in each. One cup should be ice cold, but take the ice out. The second should be room temperature. The third should be filled with hot water from the tap.

2. Set the cups on a table and let the water become still. Put a drop of food coloring gently into each cup. If you do not have food coloring, you can use another colored drink such as Kool-Aid or Gatorade to provide the color.

3. Observe the cups until the color is mixed in thoroughly. Draw a diagram similar to the one below to show how much the color mixed in each cup during the same amount of time.

Cold   Room temperature   Hot

Post-Lab Questions

1. Rank in order which cup mixed the fastest, from fastest to slowest.

2. Explain the trend based on what you know about molecules and temperature.

3. Compare what was going on in the cups to the people at a wild rock concert versus those at a calm classical music concert. You are a molecule of food coloring and everyone else is water.

ACTIVITY 26: BOILING WATER IN A SYRINGE

QUESTION

How does the boiling point of water change with pressure?

SAFETY

Use caution when working with hot tap water, as it can burn if splashed. Clean up any spills immediately.

MATERIALS

Hot water, coffee cup, syringe

PROCEDURE

The boiling point of a liquid depends on several factors. First, each substance has a unique boiling point under constant conditions. Also, contaminants can change the boiling point of a substance. Salt water has a higher boiling point than pure water. Finally, the pressure surrounding the liquid also changes the boiling point. Liquids boil when the pressure of the vibrating molecules is greater than the air pressure surrounding it. To increase the pressure of the liquid (the vapor pressure), you can heat it up. Or, by decreasing the pressure around the liquid, the boiling point can be changed because it is easier for the liquid molecules to escape. You will demonstrate that effect in this lab.

1. Put some hot tap water into a coffee cup.
2. Carefully draw water up into the syringe until it is at about 10 ml.
3. Put the cap on the syringe and slowly pull the plunger out as far as you can. Record your observations.

Post-Lab Questions
1. If the pressure in the syringe was 1.0 atm before you pulled on the plunger, what was the pressure after (in kPa)? Show your work.
2. What was the substance inside the bubbles that erupted in the liquid?
3. How is this different than the hand boiler toy in which you hold a liquid-filled glass container in your hand and the liquid begins to boil? If you have never seen a hand boiler before, you can find videos of them online.

Extensions
Experiment with this lab and see how long you can continue to make the liquid boil as the water cools. Use a table of vapor pressures and figure out how cool the water can get and still boil in the syringe. Calculate the lowest pressure you can create in the syringe and use the table of vapor pressures in your chemistry book or online to see what is the coolest temperature at which water can be boiled in the syringe.

ACTIVITY 27: LIFTING AN ICE CUBE WITH A STRING

QUESTION ❓

How does salt affect ice?

SAFETY 🩹

Dispose of all materials when finished. Do not consume any of the materials used in this activity. Clean up any spills immediately.

MATERIALS 📏

Ice cube, water, string, salt, sugar, other soluble substance

PROCEDURE 👣

In this lab, you will be shown a discrepant event (an action that does not make much sense). Then you will be asked to try to figure out how it worked. You may use your book, information given in class, and the internet to figure out your answer. Remember that the internet may contain a lot of elementary and incorrect information. If you use the internet, be careful to analyze what you read and only depend on high school–level and well-known websites. If the website is the UCLA chemistry website, it is probably trustworthy. If it is little Johnny's third-grade science fair project website, it probably is not reliable.

1. Put one large ice cube in an almost full cup of water so that it is near the top of the cup.
2. Lay a string across the top of the ice cube. Coil it in circles if possible.
3. Sprinkle salt on the string and ice cube and wait 10 sec.
4. Now lift the ice cube out of the water.
5. Try this procedure again using sugar and at least one other soluble substance. Tell whether each one had the same effect on the ice as the salt.

Wrap-Up

Write a 200-word explanation for how this event works. Try to use some of the following terms in your explanation: *freezing point depression*, *temperature*, *heat*, *heat of fusion*, *melting*, and *freezing*. As with all academic writing, spelling, grammar, and punctuation do count.

Extension

Use a similar procedure to make ice cream and consider why salt is needed in the ice in this process. Ice cream can be made using large and small zip-top bags. Find the recipe and instructions on numerous websites online. Make the ice cream only in clean kitchen containers, not containers that have been used for chemistry experiments. Research what chemicals are spread on icy roads in the winter. Is this the same process?

ACTIVITY 28: CHEMICAL FORMULA SIMULATIONS

QUESTION ❓

How is the ratio of elements in a chemical formula determined?

SAFETY 🩹

Use care in working with scissors, as they can be sharp. Keep them out of the reach of children.

MATERIALS 📏

Photocopy of Atom Cutouts page (p. 239), scissors

PROCEDURE

In this activity, you will simulate the writing of chemical formulas by cutting out some shapes and putting them together to find out how many of each it takes to completely fill up all of the connectors. This is, in a way, how ions get together to form molecules in an ionic bond. Anions get together with cations to form molecules. Anions are negative ions that have gained electrons and are represented by the consonants. Cations are positive ions that have lost electrons and are represented by the vowels. Sometimes two anions will get together and share electrons (in a covalent bond), but two cations will not form a molecule. The number of electrons that an ion wants to exchange with its partner is represented by its oxidation number or charge. The two terms are similar, and in this book, I will use *oxidation number* from now on since the word itself is not nearly as important as the concept. Some elements have different oxidation numbers under different circumstances, so to simplify this activity, you will use fake elements that always have the same oxidation number.

Keep in mind that this activity is not meant to show you physically how bonds are formed; it is simply intended to show you how to determine the chemical formula when two elements combine.

1. Roughly cut all of the pieces on page 239 (do not waste too much time trying to make them perfect).
2. Read the rules below.
3. Combine the given pieces in the combinations below and write the formula for each combination.
4. Do not throw away the pieces; you will need them again.

Here are some simple rules for combinations:

1. When combined, there should be no unused C or O in the end.
2. You may rotate, flip, and turn the pieces any way that you want. Do not cut or break them.
3. When you write the formula, the positive one (the vowel) always goes first.
4. The number of each piece in the finished product is written as a subscript number without the oxidation number. You do not need to write "1" if there is only one of a piece. For example, two A^{+1} pieces combined with one D^{-2} piece would have the formula A_2D, not A_2D_1.
5. If you can simplify by dividing both numbers by 2, do it. For example, you would not write Mg_2O_2, you would simplify it to MgO. You would not write C_2O_4; you would simplify it to CO_2.

Problems

1. Write the formula when A and C combine.
2. Write the formula when A and D combine.
3. Write the formula when A and F combine.
4. Write the formula when A and G combine.
5. Write the formula when I and B combine.

6. Write the formula when I and D combine.
7. Write the formula when I and G combine.
8. Write the formula when U and C combine.
9. Write the formula when U and F combine.
10. Write the formula when U and G combine.

Now try some real ions:

11. Write the formula when C^{+4} and H^{-1} combine.
12. Write the formula when Ca^{+2} and Cl^{-1} combine.
13. Write the formula when Na^{+1} and S^{-2} combine.
14. Write the formula when Mg^{+2} and O^{-2} combine.
15. Write the formula when Be^{+2} and N^{-3} combine.

.

ACTIVITY 29: CHEMICAL REACTION SIMULATION

How can you determine the products of a single or double displacement reaction?

Atom Cutouts page (p. 239)

In this activity, you will use the pieces that you cut out in the Chemical Formula Simulation to investigate single and double displacement reactions.

Single Displacement Reactions

A single displacement reaction is a reaction in which an element replaces an ion in a molecule. Because there is only one switch, this is called a single displacement reaction. Examples of this type of reaction are $Mg + CuCl_2 \rightarrow MgCl_2 + Cu$ and $NaI + Cl_2 \rightarrow NaCl + I_2$. In the first reaction, Mg replaced Cu, and in the second reaction, Cl replaced I. The common mistake that students make is to just put the ions together on the product side in the same proportions that they were on the reactant side.

The following is a BAD EXAMPLE ☹ $Na + MgCl_2 \rightarrow Mg + NaCl_2$ ☹. There is no such thing as $NaCl_2$. We know that the formula for table salt is NaCl, and it must be written that way. Your paper pieces will help you avoid this problem if you use them properly. Another problem that students encounter is trying to replace a positive ion with a negative one. You must always switch a positive with a positive and a negative with a negative. If you use the paper pieces correctly, you will not run into this problem either. The following is another BAD EXAMPLE ☹ : $Na + MgCl_2 \rightarrow MgNa + Cl_2$. Mg and Na are both positive ions, and they cannot make a molecule.

1. Build the molecules represented by the symbols on the reactant side of the equation and fill in the subscripts (do not write "1"s). Do not sneeze while you have them laid out!
2. Switch the appropriate ions and make sure they are full and correct. Take the reactants apart to put the products together. You will not have enough pieces for both.
3. Write the formulas of the products. Do not forget that the positive ion goes first.
4. Notice that these reactions are not always "balanced" (same number of each element on each side of the equation). You will learn how to balance equations in the next activity.

Problems

Example: $IC_2 + D \rightarrow ID + C$

1. $A + I\_F\_ \rightarrow$
2. $I\_C\_ + D \rightarrow$
3. $O + U\_D\_ \rightarrow$
4. $U\_B\_ + G \rightarrow$
5. $O + U\_G\_ \rightarrow$

Now try it with some real chemicals. Remember:

   i.   Oxidation numbers can be found on the periodic table for most ions (see the periodic table below).

   ii.   The elements H, O, F, Br, I, N, and Cl are diatomic. This means that if they are unattached to anything, they always have a 2 after them: H_2, O_2, F_2, Br_2, I_2, N_2, and Cl_2. This is only when they are unattached, not when they are part of a molecule.

   iii.   All of the rules above still apply (e.g., positive one goes first).

6. $Mg + H\_Cl\_ \rightarrow$
7. $Na\_S\_ + I_2 \rightarrow$
8. $CaO + Br_2 \rightarrow$
9. $Al\_O\_ + Ba \rightarrow$

Double Displacement Reactions

A double displacement reaction is a reaction between two molecules. In this type of reaction, the molecules switch partners. But just like before, they do not just switch, but rearrange to make the correct chemical formulas. An example is $NaI + CuCl_2 \rightarrow NaCl + CuI_2$. Notice that the Cl_2 was not simply combined with the Na, because there's no such thing as $NaCl_2$. The correct formula for the products must be written and the paper pieces will help you do that. It does not matter if you switch the positive ion or the negative ion; you will get the correct answer as long as you write the positive ion first.

Problems

Example: $IC_2 + EB \rightarrow OB_2 + EC$

10. $E\_D\_ + I\_C\_ \rightarrow$
11. $A\_D\_ + I\_F\_ \rightarrow$
12. $O\_C\_ + E\_D\_ \rightarrow$
13. $U\_G\_ + E\_C\_ \rightarrow$
14. $O\_F\_ + I\_G\_ \rightarrow$

Now try it with some real chemicals, and remember the following:

    i.   You cannot do these if you do not know the oxidation numbers of the ions, so first look them up on the periodic table provided.
    ii. Do not just put them together as is. Write the correct formulas.
    iii. Positive ions go first.

Problems

15. $NaCl + CaI_2 \rightarrow$
16. $KNO_3 + LiF \rightarrow$
17. $H_2SO_4 + Li_2O \rightarrow$
18. $Fe_2O_3 + NaOH \rightarrow$
19. $CuSO_4 + HNO_3 \rightarrow$

General Trend for Oxidation Numbers

+1																	0
H	+2											+3	+/-4	-3	-2	-1	He
Li	Be											B	C	N	O	F	Ne
Na	Mg				Multiple oxidative states							Al	Si	P	S	Cl	Ar
K	Ca	Sc	Ti	V	Or	Mn	Fe	Co	Ni	Cu	Zn	Ga	Ge	As	Se	Br	Kr
Rb	Sr	Y	Zr	No	Mo	Tc	Ru	Ph	Pd	Ag	Cd	In	Sn	Sb	Te	I	Xe
Cs	Ba	La	Hf	Ta	W	Re	Os	Ir	Pt	Au	Hg	TL	Pb	Bi	Po	At	Rn
Fr	Rd	Ac															

ACTIVITY 30: BALANCING CHEMICAL EQUATIONS SIMULATION

QUESTION ?

How is the law of conservation of matter shown in a balanced chemical reaction?

MATERIALS

Atom Cutout page (p. 239), scissors

PROCEDURE

In the last simulation, you used papers to represent chemical reactions. But many of the reactions that you wrote violated the law of conservation of matter, which states that matter can not be created or destroyed. That means if you have two carbon atoms before a reaction, you must have two carbon atoms after the reaction. If you look at the example from the last simulation, this law was violated.

$$IC_2 + EB \rightarrow IB_2 + EC$$

It is important to know that the chemicals on the left side of the reaction arrow are called reactants and the chemicals on the right side of the reaction arrow are called products.

In the reactant, there were two Cs. But in the product there was only one. That violates the law of conservation of matter. To fix this, we have to "balance" the equation. One way to balance this equation would be to write it like this:

$$\text{☹} \quad IC_2 + EB_2 \rightarrow IB_2 + EC_2 \quad \text{☹}$$

(NOTE: THIS IS AN EXAMPLE OF WHAT NOT TO DO.)

But there is no such thing as EB_2 and there is no such thing as EC_2. Those formulas are written incorrectly. You can add more of each compound by putting coefficients in front of each compound in the equation.

$IC_2 + 2EB \rightarrow IB_2 + 2EC$

Now there is one I on the left and one on the right. There are two Cs on the left and two on the right. There are two Es on the left and two on the right. There are two Bs on the left and two on the right. You are allowed to add more chemicals; you just cannot change the formula of the chemicals.

With your element cutouts, the equation would look like this:

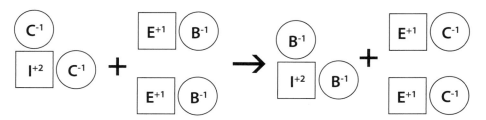

Now use your pieces to balance the following equations following these rules:

a. All of the compounds must be built correctly.
b. The number of each element must be equal on both sides of the reaction arrow.
c. The number of each element is written before the chemical formula in the balanced equation and is a full-size number, not subscript.

    An extra sheet of elements is included here because you will certainly need them. As you go along, you might not need to build the chemicals any more to get the answer, but be sure to check your answer when you are finished.

1. I_C_ + D →
2. O + U_D_ →
3. U_B_ + G →
4. A_D_ + I_F_ →
5. O_C_ + E_D_ →
6. U_G_ + E_C_ →

Now try it with real chemicals:

   a. Assign oxidation numbers to each atom.
   b. Determine what type of reaction it is (e.g., single displacement, double displacement, etc.).
   c. Finish the equation.
   d. Balance the equation.

   7. $CaCl_2 + Na \rightarrow$
   8. $KF + O_2 \rightarrow$
   9. $CuI_2 + LiBr \rightarrow$
  10. $MgO + HCl \rightarrow$
  11. $H_2 + O_2 \rightarrow$
  12. $Al + Cl2 \rightarrow$

ACTIVITY 31: MOLECULAR SHAPE

QUESTION ❓

How does the shape of a molecule affect its chemical properties?

SAFETY

Clean up any spilled or splashed water when finished to avoid slipping.

MATERIALS

Comb, balloon, or other source of static electricity; water faucet

PROCEDURE

Because oxygen has six valence electrons (Figure 1), it bonds with two hydrogen atoms, each having one valence electron. But there are two different configurations that this combination could make. The hydrogen atoms could line up across from each other (Figure 2), or they could arrange themselves next to each other (Figure 3).

:Ö·
·
H·

H:Ö:H

:Ö:H
Ḧ

Figure 1   Figure 2   Figure 3

The way to tell which configuration the water molecule actually takes the form of is to test its properties. In the configuration in Figure 2, the hydrogen atoms are slightly positive because the oxygen atom is pulling on the electrons harder than the hydrogen atom. Therefore, each end of the molecule is positive and water would not be affected by static electricity. In the configuration in Figure 3, the hydrogen atoms are both on the same side and two pairs of electrons (negative) are on the other side. This would make the water molecule have poles like a magnet, and it would be affected by static electricity.

1. Test whether a thin stream of water from a faucet is affected by static electricity or not.
2. Static electricity can be generated in many ways. Be sure that the object is charged by showing that hair is attracted to it.

    a. Rub a balloon on your hair or a pet's hair.
    b. Comb your hair with a plastic comb.

Post-Lab Questions
1. What happened, if anything, when you brought the static electricity near the stream of water?
2. Which figure (p. 159) shows the actual structure of water?
3. Molecules that have a partial positive charge on one end and a partial negative charge on the other end are said to be polar. Molecules that have the same charge on both ends are called nonpolar. Is water polar or nonpolar?

Extension
Test the effect of static electricity on small, light objects, such as scraps of paper, salt, pepper, tiny pieces of aluminum foil, and sugar. Were any of them not attracted to the charged object? What can you say about their molecular structures? Wear goggles if you use any dangerous materials.

ACTIVITY 32: IDENTIFYING TYPES OF STREETLIGHTS LAB

QUESTION ?

How can you determine what type of bulb is in a streetlight?

SAFETY

Be sure to stay out of traffic when looking in the spectroscope at night. Do not point the spectroscope at the sun. Be careful with scissors.

MATERIALS

Shoe box, CD, scissors

PROCEDURE

In this lab, you will use a diffraction grating to determine what type of lightbulb is used in a nearby parking lot. You will be provided with a card, given access to a card, or directed to a website that has the different spectra for the different types of lights used in outdoor lighting (high-pressure sodium, fluorescent, etc.). This process is called spectroscopy. Spectroscopy is often used in astronomy, chemistry, and physics, and even was used for discovering the double-helix structure of DNA.

Constructing the Spectroscope

Colored light is created when electrons are bumped up to higher energy levels and drop back down. Different elements have different energy levels, so they each give off different colors when they light up. The different colors of light that an element gives off are called its emission spectrum, which is important in chemistry. The emission spectrum is used to recognize unknown elements, identify the elements in a star, and determine how fast a galaxy is moving.

You will use a CD as the diffraction grating in your spectroscope. It does not matter what type of CD you use—computer, music, or AOL discs would all work. If you have one of the clear CDs that come as spacers when you buy recordable CDs, read the alternate directions below (the clear CD must show a rainbow when you look at it in the light).

In one end of a shoe box or similar container, poke or cut a hole about the size of a penny. At the other end, use tape to put the CD inside the box at an angle and cut a slit in the box above the CD. Tape the lid on so that light cannot get in from the sides.

Take your spectroscope to the parking lot chosen by your teacher, and look at the lights through the spectroscope. Make sure to be as far as possible from any other sources of light, such as headlights and neon signs. Draw a sketch of the brightly colored lines that you see and label the colors of the lines. Now repeat this with another type of light on the street or in another parking lot. You will be told where to find the information to tell what kinds of lights they are.

Post-Lab Questions

1. What was the most difficult part about determining what type of light you used?
2. How sure were you that you got the right one?
3. Why did you have to put a slit in the box instead of just leaving off the top?

ACTIVITY 33: GROWING CRYSTALS

QUESTION ❓

How are crystals of different chemicals similar and different?

SAFETY 🩹

Use only hot tap water; do not heat water in a microwave or on the stove. Do not eat any of the crystals or other materials during this activity, as mold quickly grows on some of the crystals. Mark the cups clearly and keep them out of the reach of children. Clean up spills immediately.

MATERIALS 📏

Cups, water, sugar, salt, Epsom salt, thread

PROCEDURE 👣

In this lab, you will grow three different types of crystals: sugar, salt, and Epsom salts. Crystals are grown by either dissolving more material than the solvent can normally hold by heating it, or by allowing the solvent to evaporate over time. In this procedure, you will do a little of both. You will put a lot of solute in a little solvent and heat it to dissolve; then you will let it sit for a few days to evaporate.

1. For each of the solutes, dissolve a large spoonful in about 30 ml of hot tap water. Stir until all of the solute is gone.

2. Once all of the solute has dissolved, transfer the solution to a disposable cup, leaving any undissolved solid behind. Hang a short thread in the solution. If the string will not sink, you can tie a paper clip to the end. Allow it to sit on a windowsill for several days while the water evaporates. Pull the string out and let the crystals dry overnight. Record observations of your crystals every day and include the number of crystals, size, shape, and other characteristics. Put the crystals in labeled zip-top bags and carefully take them to school to turn in.
3. Find a good example of each crystal and sketch its shape. Try to find a single crystal without other crystals growing out of it. If your crystals are small, you can look at them under a magnifying glass.

Post-Lab Questions
1. Which substance grew the largest crystals?
2. How would you describe the shape of each crystal?
3. If equal masses of each substance were used, then the one with the lowest molar mass would have contained the largest number of molecules of that substance and would have the highest concentration. The highest concentration should grow the fastest but will produce the smallest crystals. Use the formulas to determine if your crystals followed this pattern: $NaCl$, $C_6H_{12}O_6$, and $MgSO_4$. Did the substance with the highest molar mass grow the largest crystals?

ACTIVITY 34: DECOMPOSITION OF WATER LAB

QUESTION

Which gas forms at which electrode during electrolysis?

SAFETY

Goggles are required for this activity. If the wires are connected together (shorted), the battery can get hot and leak caustic chemicals. Do not use a leaking battery. Be careful not to let the battery touch anything metal when it is put back in the box. Do not leave the experiment running for long periods of time. Disconnect if the battery or wires get hot. Be careful with wires, as they can be sharp.

MATERIALS

Glass, water, 9 V battery, wires or battery clip, pencil lead, pinch of salt

PROCEDURE

Electricity can be used to decompose water into hydrogen gas and oxygen gas according to this balanced equation: $2H_2O_{(l)} \rightarrow 2H_{2(g)} + O_{2(g)}$.

Decomposition is a type of chemical reaction in which a large molecule breaks up into two or more smaller molecules. According to this equation, during the decomposition of water, twice as much hydrogen as oxygen will be created. You will use this fact to determine whether the hydrogen builds up at the positive or negative side of the battery. You will then determine which pole of the battery is the anode and which is the cathode. The anode is the pole to which negative ions are attracted. Oxygen will be produced at the anode. The cathode is the pole to which positive ions are attracted. Hydrogen will be produced at the cathode.

1. Using a piece of tape, attach the wires from the battery clip to a piece of graphite (mechanical pencil lead). Be sure the wires are touching the graphite before you seal the tape. Any kind of tape will work. Try to leave as much of the graphite exposed as possible and cover the exposed wire with tape.
2. Attach the battery clip to the battery. If you are using bare wires instead of a clip, make sure the red wire comes from the positive terminal and the black wire comes from the negative terminal.
3. Prepare a small cup with 50 ml of water. To ensure that the water will conduct electricity, add a pinch of salt to the water and stir.
4. Lower the graphite electrodes into the salt water, but do not allow the tape and wires to go into the water. If nothing happens, gently squeeze the tape to make sure that the wires are touching the graphite. Check that the battery is not dead by putting it into a device that uses 9 V batteries. Add a little more salt and stir the water. Move the electrodes closer together.
5. Watch the production of bubbles and notice which electrode is producing bubbles faster. Record your observations in your lab notebook.

Post-Lab Questions
1. Which electrode bubbled faster, the one connected to the red wire or the black wire?
2. Which gas was being produced slowly? Which was being produced quickly?
3. Why did the wire identified in #1 bubble more quickly? Use terms such as *balanced equation*, *products*, *reactants*, *moles*, and *decomposition* in your explanation.

Extension
Research Pons and Fleischmann's cold fusion experiment and see how they used electrolysis for their discovery. Was their cold fusion discovery discredited because of the science or because of the way they reported the science?

ACTIVITY 35: SOLUBILITY LAB

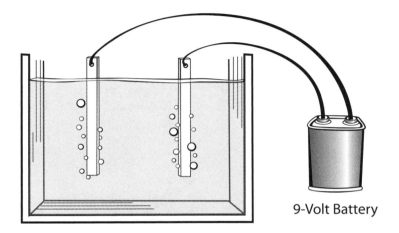

9-Volt Battery

QUESTION

Which household substances are polar and which are nonpolar?

SAFETY

Wear goggles during this activity. Keep the cups out of the reach of children so they do not drink the solutions. Do not consume any of the materials. Use caution when working with rubbing alcohol; it is flammable. Keep away from all flames and/or spark sources. Immediately wipe up any liquid spilled on the floor.

MATERIALS

6 cups, oil, water, rubbing alcohol, salt, sugar, baking soda

PROCEDURE

In this lab, you will figure out which solids are soluble in which liquids. For the liquids, you will use water, rubbing alcohol, and cooking oil. For the solids, you will use salt, sugar, and baking soda. In the end, you will see if the liquids will mix together. This will help you answer the question about which solutes and solvents are polar.

In a small cup, try the following combinations to see if the solute will dissolve in the solvent. Stir the solutions and allow at least 60 sec. for the solutes to dissolve. Be sure to clean the cups with dishwashing liquid between each use.

1. water and salt
2. water and sugar
3. water and baking soda
4. rubbing alcohol and salt
5. rubbing alcohol and sugar
6. rubbing alcohol and baking soda
7. cooking oil and salt
8. cooking oil and sugar
9. cooking oil and baking soda
10. cooking oil and water

Post-Lab Questions

1. In general, polar items dissolve other polar items and nonpolar items dissolve nonpolar items. Water is polar. Which of the solids are polar?
2. In general, polar liquids mix with other polar liquids, and vice versa. Which of the liquids are polar?
3. From your experience, is antifreeze polar? Epsom salts? Car oil? Animal fat? NutraSweet? Sand?

ACTIVITY 36: SEA ICE LAB

When ice forms in salt water, is the ice salty or not?

Clean up any spills immediately. Do not eat or drink any of the materials.

Water, plastic cup, salt

Sea ice is different from glaciers. Glaciers are formed when years and years of snow accumulate in a very cold place and then pieces break off and float away. Because glaciers are formed by precipitation, they are made of freshwater. Sea ice forms when it gets cold enough over the ocean that a layer of ocean water freezes. In this activity, you will determine whether or not sea ice is salty.

To tell if water is salty or not, you will simply put a few drops on a surface and allow it to evaporate. If it is salty, you will see salt left over after the water is all gone. Evaporating the water on dark-colored paper makes it very easy to see. Some tap water has lots of solids dissolved in it, so it is better to use bottled water. Try to evaporate some tap water first to see what it looks like.

1. Put 30 ml of water in the small plastic cup and add a spoonful of salt. Stir until all of the salt is gone and the solution is clear.
2. Evaporate some of this water to test for saltiness.
3. Place the salt water in the freezer and check on it every 10 min.

4. Once a layer of ice about 0.50 cm thick has formed, take the salt water out of the freezer and remove the layer of ice. Do not let the entire cup freeze.
5. Rinse the ice with water momentarily to get any salt water off its surface.
6. Allow some of the ice to melt, then test the melted ice for saltiness.
7. Test the leftover water in the cup for saltiness.

Post-Lab Questions
1. Which of the samples had the highest level of saltiness: the original salt water, the ice, or the leftover water? Which had the lowest level?
2. In class, you will learn about freezing point depression. When you do, calculate the freezing point of ocean water given that 1,000 g of salt water has 37 g of salt in it and the freezing point depression constant of water is 1.86°C/mol. Do not forget that there will be two ions present, not just one.
3. Give your hypothesis for how the ice ended up the way that it did. Try to include as many of these terms as possible: *concentration, salinity, freezing point depression, temperature, solute, solvent, liquid,* and *solid*.

Extension
There are a couple of common myths about freezing and boiling that may or may not be true. Investigate them. The first myth is that if you put a cup of hot water and a cup of room temperature water in the freezer, the hot water will freeze first. The second myth is that a pinch of salt in boiling water will make pasta or vegetables cook faster. For safety reasons, only boil water with adult supervision.

ACTIVITY 37: INVISIBLE INK LAB

QUESTION

What chemical makes invisible ink work?

SAFETY

Use goggles for this activity because most of the chemicals can hurt your eyes. Do not eat or drink any of the materials. Clean up any spills.

MATERIALS

Students determine what materials to use.

PROCEDURE

One way to make an invisible ink is to write on a piece of paper with the juice from a fruit and let it dry. Then heating it above a toaster or with a hair dryer will make the writing visible. But what chemical in the fruit juice makes the color change? This is what you will attempt to figure out in this activity.

First, make sure that you can do the demonstration with a liquid known to work. Use a stick or a cotton swab to write something on a piece of scratch paper (do not waste a new piece of paper) with lemon, apple, or pineapple juice. If the juice does not come straight from the fruit, be sure to make sure there is real fruit juice in it. Many fruit drinks that you buy in the store do not really have any fruit juice in them. (Strange, isn't it?)

Allow the juice to dry until it is invisible. Hold the paper 2 in. above a toaster (holding the edges of the paper so you do not burn yourself), hold it over a lightbulb, or put it 2 in. in front of a hair dryer. Watch for a couple of minutes to see if the invisible ink becomes visible. If it does not, keep trying until you can see it before you start your investigation.

Now that you can get invisible ink to turn visible, you will try to figure out what is in the liquid you used that made the ink show up when heated. When you have a hypothesis for what chemical it might be, make up a solution of that chemical and test it. For example, if you believe that salt is what turns colors, test some salt water using the same procedure you did for the fruit juice. Try testing other liquids that have similar chemicals and different chemicals.

Keep a list of the liquids that you tested and a description of the results similar to the chart below:

Fruit Juice	Observations
Liquid 1	
Liquid 2	
Liquid 3	

Post-Lab Questions

1. Which liquids made successful invisible inks? Which liquids did not?
2. What did the successful liquids all have in them that the unsuccessful liquids did not?
3. What did your experiments tell you is in the fruit juice that makes it a good invisible ink? Explain your thought process as you came to this conclusion. Use statements such as "Because _____ and _____ happened, I eliminated _____. Because _____ and _____ were successful, I decided to test _____. And because _____ happened, I conclude that the chemical that makes fruit juice work as an invisible ink is _____."

SECTION 3:
Chemical Reactions

ACTIVITY 38: OXIDATION LAB

Objective
Students will put two different types of nails (galvanized and nongalvanized) into different conditions to see how the rate of rusting is affected.

Topic: Oxidation
Go to: *www.scilinks.org*
Code: THC31

Purpose
Students will see how moisture, anodizing, and salt affect the rusting of a nail.

Materials
2 galvanized nails, 2 standard nails (Home Depot calls them bright), 2 paper towels, water, salt

Notes
It is sometimes difficult to find nails that have not somehow been modified to prevent rust. They will be slightly cheaper than other nails. The size of the nail does not matter much. Other variables you can test are scratching through the zinc layer of a galvanized nail, spraying with rust-proof paint, using tap water versus distilled water, or testing aluminum versus iron.

Post-Lab Questions
1. Because salt contributes to rust. A boat that has been in salt water is more likely than the trailer and bearings to have rust damage.
2. Gold is very resistant to oxidation (rust), which is why it is used in electronics. Gold is less conductive than both aluminum and copper, but when aluminum and copper oxidize, they lose their conductivity very quickly.
3. The salt gets kicked up onto the undercarriage of the car and causes rust.

ACTIVITY 39: SYNTHESIS REACTION

Objective
Students will put a penny in ammonia and observe it for several days.

Purpose
Students will perform a synthesis reaction and observe the properties of the complex formed.

Materials
Plastic cup, ammonia, clean penny

Notes
Results on this lab can vary slightly because of other characteristics that manufacturers add to their ammonia, such as soap, fragrance, and color. Distilled vinegar works best, but some students will use whatever they have at home. Most students will see the blue color of the complex. Some ammonia is colored yellow and the solution comes out green. The small amount of complex made in this lab can be rinsed down the drain for disposal or dried and put into the trash in most areas. Check local regulations for differences in policy.

Post-Lab Questions
1. $Cu + 4NH_3 \rightarrow Cu(NH_4)_4^{+2}$
2. Blue or blue green
3. Some say that it got shiny; others say that it changed colors.

SC_INKS_
THE WORLD'S A CLICK AWAY

Topic: Reaction Types
Go to: *www.scilinks.org*
Code: THC32

ACTIVITY 40: SINGLE DISPLACEMENT REACTION

Objective
Students will use steel wool and vinegar to form iron (II) acetate.

Purpose
Students will perform a single displacement reaction and collect the products to be used in another lab.

Materials
Cup, steel wool, vinegar

Notes
There are many types of vinegar (apple cider, red wine, etc.) that can affect the results of this experiment. It will work with any of the vinegar varieties, but colors can be different. Encourage students to use standard clear vinegar (distilled vinegar). I cannot tell you how many students have told me, "My mom thought it was trash and threw it away." Make sure the whole family knows what is going on, or else this lab and the next one will be ruined. Some steel wool comes coated with oil or other materials to prevent rust while on the store shelf. Test your steel wool before distributing it, and clean it with rubbing alcohol if it does not work properly.

Post-Lab Questions
1. $Fe + 2HC_2H_3O_2 \rightarrow Fe(C_2H_3O_2)_2 + H_2$
2. Soluble in water, color, etc.
3. Hydrogen was the other product and most students notice the bubbles.

SC**LINKS**
THE WORLD'S A CLICK AWAY

Topic: Factors Affecting Reaction Rate
Go to: *www.scilinks.org*
Code: THC33

ACTIVITY 41: DOUBLE DISPLACEMENT REACTION: PRECIPITATE LAB

Objective

Students will mix ammonia with the iron (II) acetate from Activity 40 to make a precipitate.

Purpose

Students will learn about solubility and precipitates by performing a double displacement reaction.

Materials

Iron (II) acetate (Activity 40), ammonia, zip-top bag

Notes

Some students do not have any ammonia at home. The color of the precipitate can vary due to the type of vinegar used in Activity 40. The mass of precipitate also will vary based on how much steel wool was used and how long each reaction is allowed to proceed.

Post-Lab Questions

1. $NH_4C_2H_3O_2$
2. The iron (II) acetate was all used up.
3. Because it seems to be falling down like rain or snow, which are called precipitation

Safety

If you are going to give students ammonia to take home, use only household ammonia. Send it in a well-sealed container that is carefully marked according to the standards your state requires. Remove the label from the bottle and write on it with a permanent marker. Students should also carefully mark the iron (II) acetate and the iron (II) hydroxide. Iron (II) hydroxide is a base.

SC*L*INKS.
THE WORLD'S A CLICK AWAY

Topic: Precipitation Reactions
Go to: *www.scilinks.org*
Code: THC34

ACTIVITY 38: OXIDATION LAB

QUESTION ❓

What keeps metals from rusting?

SAFETY

Keep these materials out of the reach of small children. Be careful not to scratch yourself with a rusty nail. Wear goggles when working with the nails.

MATERIALS

2 galvanized nails, 2 standard nails (Home Depot calls them bright), 2 paper towels, water, salt

PROCEDURE

In this lab, you will test different items to see if they inhibit rust. You will take two iron nails and two galvanized (zinc-coated) nails and put them under different conditions to see how much rust forms. Keep them moist with tap water or salt water and roll them over daily.

- Nail A: Leave iron nail (shiny) A between two moist paper towels and do not let it dry out.
- Nail B: Leave galvanized nail (dull gray) B between two moist paper towels and do not let it dry out.
- Nail C: Leave iron nail (shiny) C between two paper towels moistened with salt water and do not let it dry out.
- Nail D: Leave galvanized nail (dull gray) D between two paper towels moistened with salt water and do not let it dry out.

Each day for two weeks, record observations about the nails in your notebooks. When rust begins to form, rank the nails from 1 to 4, with 1 being the least rusty and 4 being the most rusty.

Post-Lab Questions

1. Why is it that when people sell boats, they often say, "Has never been in salt water"?
2. People think electronics are coated with gold because it is a good conductor of electricity, but that is not the reason. Does this lab give you another idea? Have you ever seen rusty gold?
3. In cold climates, people spread salt to melt ice and prevent slippery roads. How could this be bad for cars?

ACTIVITY 39: SYNTHESIS REACTION

QUESTION ❓

How do you predict the products of a synthesis reaction?

SAFETY

Wear goggles at all times when handling these chemicals. Label this experiment carefully and keep it out of reach of children. If you get ammonia on your skin, rinse it off thoroughly under running water. If you get ammonia in your eyes, rinse them under warm water for 15 minutes.

MATERIALS

Plastic cup, ammonia, clean penny

PROCEDURE

A synthesis reaction is one in which two small elements or compounds combine to form one larger, more complex compound. An example would be when carbon and oxygen combine to form carbon dioxide: $C_{(s)} + O_{2(g)} \rightarrow CO_{2(g)}$. In this reaction, you will form a complex that contains one copper atom and four amine ions: $Cu(NH_3)_4^{+2}$. Complexes are often very colorful, as you will see. Note that the (s) and (g) in the chemical equation simply mean solid or gas.

1. Since you will let this experiment sit for many days, do not use a paper cup or the liquids will soak through. Pour household ammonia into the plastic cup until it is approximately 1.0 cm deep.
2. Put a clean penny in the cup and either put a lid on the cup or cover it with plastic wrap. Do not cover it with aluminum foil or you could get some unexpected reactions between the ammonia and the aluminum.
3. Make daily observations of the penny and the ammonia for seven days.

Observations

Day	Penny Observations	Ammonia Observations
1		
2		
3		
4		
5		
6		
7		

Post-Lab Questions

1. Write and balance the equation for the formation of the colored complex from the information given in the introduction.
2. What color was the copper complex (the complex is soluble in water and will be in the liquid, not on the penny or at the bottom of the cup)?
3. What happened to the penny throughout this experiment?

Extension

Use the internet to investigate methods for chemically cleaning pennies. Write chemical equations for each of the reactions. What type of reactions are they? Try them if the chemicals are not dangerous.

ACTIVITY 40: SINGLE DISPLACEMENT REACTION

QUESTION ❓

How can the products of a single displacement reaction be predicted?

SAFETY 🔲

Goggles are required for this activity. Keep all materials out of the reach of small children. Label the experiment carefully so that it does not get discarded or ingested. If you get vinegar on your skin or in your eyes, rinse with warm water for 15 minutes.

MATERIALS 📏

Cup, steel wool, vinegar

PROCEDURE 👣

A single displacement reaction occurs when an element replaces part of another compound and releases it. When a metal reacts with an acid, a single displacement reaction has taken place: $Mg_{(s)} + 2HCl_{(aq)} \rightarrow MgCl_{2(aq)} + H_{2(g)}$. In this experiment, you will use steel wool (which contains iron) and vinegar (acetic acid, $HC_2H_3O_2$). One of the products of this reaction is iron (II) acetate: $Fe(C_2H_3O_2)_2$. *Note:* $_{(s)}$ means solid, $_{(aq)}$ means aqueous or dissolved in water, and $_{(g)}$ means gas.

1. You will let this experiment run for several days, so use a glass jar or plastic cup, not a paper cup. Pour enough vinegar in the cup to make the liquid 2.0 cm deep.

2. Put a wad of steel wool about the size of a large marble (2.0 cm diameter) in the vinegar. The wool should be completely covered by the vinegar. Do not use all of the steel wool because you need more later.
3. Observe the steel wool and the vinegar for 7 days.
4. Discard the remaining steel wool from the cup and save the solution for the next experiment. Label the container so that it does not get thrown away.

Observations

Day	Steel Wool Observations	Vinegar Observations
1		
2		
3		
4		
5		
6		
7		

Post-Lab Questions

1. Write the balanced equation for the formation of the iron (II) acetate.
2. Name two properties of iron (II) acetate.
3. What was the other product of this reaction? Were you able to see it?

ACTIVITY 41: DOUBLE DISPLACEMENT REACTION: PRECIPITATE LAB

QUESTION

Where does the precipitate come from in some double displacement reactions?

SAFETY

Goggles are required for this activity. Label this experiment carefully and keep out of the reach of children. Iron (II) hydroxide is a base. If it comes in contact with the skin, wash thoroughly with water. If the chemicals make contact with the eyes, rinse with running water for 15 minutes.

MATERIALS

Iron (II) acetate (Activity 40), ammonia, zip-top bag

PROCEDURE

A double displacement reaction is one in which the ions in two compounds switch places. For example, $NaCl + AgNO_3 \rightarrow NaNO_3 + AgCl$ is a double displacement reaction because the $Na+$ and the $Ag+$ ions switched places. In this lab, you will use the solution from the last experiment to perform a double displacement reaction with ammonia. It is important to know that ammonia (NH_3), when added to water, acts like NH_4OH in the form of ($NH_3 + H_2O \rightarrow NH_4OH$). There is debate about whether NH_4OH actually exists, but chemical reactions occur as though it does and that is what is important here.

Often, a precipitate forms in a double displacement reaction. If one of the products of the reaction is not soluble in water, it will form a powder that settles to the bottom of the container like snow. That powder is called a precipitate in chemistry.

1. Take the iron (II) acetate solution from the last experiment and slowly add ammonia drop by drop until a green precipitate forms.
2. Keep adding the ammonia until no more precipitate forms.
3. Let the precipitate settle to the bottom and then carefully pour off the liquid without losing any of the precipitate. This is called decanting. Let the precipitate dry out and then put it in a zip-top bag to take to school so you can find its mass.

Post-Lab Questions
1. If the formula of the precipitate was $Fe(OH)_2$, what was the other product in the reaction between the $Fe(C_2H_3O_2)_2$ and the NH_4OH?
2. Why did the precipitate stop forming after a while? Explain.
3. Why do you think that this type of reaction is called a precipitate reaction?

Extension
As you recall, dissolved chemicals cannot be filtered out, but precipitates can. Do some research to find out some pollutants in lakes and rivers and see if there is a chemical that could precipitate the pollutants out. Is the chemical used to precipitate dangerous to the wildlife in the ecosystem? Would the precipitate cause any harm?

SECTION 4:

Gas Laws, pH, and Kinetic Molecular Theory

ACTIVITY 42: CARTESIAN DIVER LAB

Objective
Students will make a Cartesian diver out of a mustard packet and paper clip.

Purpose
Students will learn that density and buoyancy depend on both mass and volume. They will also experience that an increase in pressure (squeezing the bottle) decreases the volume of a gas (shrinks the air bubble in the mustard packet) and increases its density (same mass, smaller volume).

Materials
2 L soda bottle, mustard packet, paper clip, water, syringe

Notes
Many websites say you can do this lab with packets of ketchup. After collecting 200 packets of ketchup, I found that only a few of them worked. Many ketchup packets would sink right away and others would not sink, no matter how hard you squeezed. Jack in the Box ketchup seemed to be the only packets that worked by themselves. Soy sauce packets and vinegar packets did not work either. Mustard packets were perfect because the addition of the paper clip helps students see the relationship to mass and the transparency of one side of the packet allows students to see the bubble get smaller.

Because the masses of mustard packets and paper clips are small, you may want to give students the masses instead of having them try to measure the items with their balance.

Post-Lab Questions
1. Answers will vary but should be around 6.0 ml.
2. The density must be the same as the water, approximately 1.0 g/ml.
3. No, the mass does not change.
4. Equal in number to the mass, or approximately 5.7 ml
5. Without the paper clip, the density could not be raised enough, no matter how small the air bubble became.

SC*i*
*L*INKS.
THE WORLD'S A CLICK AWAY

Topic: Buoyancy
Go to: *www.scilinks.org*
Code: THC35

ACTIVITY 43: PRESSURE LAB

Objective

Students will see a card held up by atmospheric pressure when water and a partial vacuum are above it.

Topic: Atmospheric Pressure
Go to: *www.scilinks.org*
Code: THC23

Purpose

Students will practice calculating pressure and see how differences in pressure between two sides of an object can create a force.

Materials

Drinking glass, water, 3 × 5 in. card, ruler

Notes

Many students have never seen this demonstration before. When seeing this for the first time, students will have more difficulty figuring out the explanation than students who have seen it before. For an added flair, there is a magic trick available that allows you to perform this feat and then remove the card without the water falling out. The metal cup has a rim and a false bottom that falls down and plugs the mouth of the cup. This is a good discrepant event to challenge students' reasoning skills. The teacher can decide whether or not the students are ready for discrepant events.

Post-Lab Questions

1. The air pushing up is pushing harder. An atmosphere of air pushes harder than a few inches of water.
2. Because the air is pushing up harder than the water is pushing down. The card makes it so that air cannot sneak in from one side as it would if the card was not there.
3. Normal air pressure is approximately 15 pounds per square inch. The piece of paper is 93.5 square inches. The pressure pushing up on the paper is 1,400 pounds.

ACTIVITY 44: BOYLE'S LAW LAB

Objective
Students will see how different objects act when placed under pressures higher and lower than atmospheric pressure.

SCI **LINKS**
THE WORLD'S A CLICK AWAY

Topic: Atmospheric Pressure
Go to: *www.scilinks.org*
Code: THC23

Purpose
Students will observe Boyle's law by seeing that gases get smaller under high pressure and larger under low pressure.

Materials
Syringe, water, marshmallows, soda

Notes
This lab is simple yet powerful. Even after calculations and demonstrations, students still have trouble remembering the inverse relationship between pressure and volume. They sometimes think pressure is how hard the gas pushes, and the harder the gas pushes, the larger the gas wants to become. Instead, this lab shows students that pressure is being applied to the gas, and the more pressure is applied, the smaller the volume of the gas becomes. Use the small marshmallows, not the large ones. Large ones will get lodged inside the syringes and make a sticky mess. Pass the marshmallows out just before the activity so they do not become hard.

Questions
Q1: Answers will vary, but should be around 5 ml.
Q2: Answers will vary, but are usually all the way out to 60 ml.
Q3: Not at all.
Q4: Gases.
Q5: It gets bigger.
Q6: It gets smaller.

Q7: Increasing the pressure on the bubbles in the marshmallow causes the volume to decrease. Decreasing the pressure causes the volume to increase. Some of the bubbles near the outside of the marshmallow will pop, so the marshmallow will look different after the experiment.

Q8: The bubbles do not form as fast, and the ones that already exist get smaller.

Q9: The bubbles form quickly and get bigger.

Q10: Increasing the pressure decreases the bubbles' volume. Decreasing the pressure increases the bubbles' volume. (Note: In more advanced classes, you may want to talk about the equilibrium of increasing the pressure on a reaction that involves gases [$H_2CO_3 \rightarrow H_2O + CO_2$], Le Chatlier's Principle.)

ACTIVITY 45: FINGER THERMOMETER

Objective
Students will attempt to estimate the temperature of objects by touching them.

Purpose
Students will see that human skin is not good at judging absolute temperature, only relative temperatures. Knowing the difference between absolute measurements and relative measurements is a powerful skill on its own.

Materials
3 cups with cold water, room temperature water, and warm water

Post-Lab Questions
1. The water feels hot to the left hand and cold to the right hand.
2. No, the skin cannot tell the actual temperature of objects, only relative temperature.
3. The nerves in the hand and the nerves in the eye get used to a situation and then react strangely to a change in the situation.

Topic: Temperature and Regulation
Go to: *www.scilinks.org*
Code: THC36

ACTIVITY 46: EXPANSION AND CONTRACTION

Objective
Students will measure the expansion and contraction of a balloon as it is cooled and heated.

Purpose
Students will observe Charles' law by measuring the volume of cold, warm, and hot balloons.

Materials
Small balloon, small bucket, water, large container, syringe, tongs or stick

Notes
Although Charles' law cannot be verified quantitatively with this lab, the direct relationship between temperature and volume can clearly be seen. The temperatures are not known exactly but can be approximated. The elastic forces of the balloon will not allow quantitative measurements to be made. A large zip-top bag would be better if quantitative results are desired. Freezers are in the range of 265°K. Refrigerators are in the range of 285°K. Room temperature is about 300°K and hot water is about 350°K. So the difference between the lowest (freezer) and highest (hot water) should be about 35%.

Post-Lab Questions
1. Smaller; answers will vary.
2. Answers will vary, but students should draw a graph with temperature on the horizontal axis and volume on the vertical axis. Where the volume is zero is the estimate for absolute zero. Because of all the assumptions in this lab, the answers may not be close, but the process of estimating absolute zero should be clear.
3. Water with a temperature similar to the balloon's was used to avoid changing the temperature of the balloon before the volume could be measured.

SCi LINKS.
THE WORLD'S A CLICK AWAY

Topic: Heat and Temperature
Go to: *www.scilinks.org*
Code: THC37

ACTIVITY 47: pH PAPER LAB

Objective
Students will use homemade pH paper to test a number of chemicals around the house.

Topic: pH
Go to: *www.scilinks.org*
Code: THC38

Purpose
Students will learn what chemicals around them are considered acids and bases and estimate the chemicals' pH values.

Materials
pH paper made from paper towels and red (purple) cabbage juice

Notes
To make the pH paper, just cut up a head of red cabbage and boil the color out of it. Strain out the solids and allow the liquid to cool. Dip long strips of white paper towel or coffee filter (approximately 20 cm) into the liquid and lay them out to dry. If the color is not dark enough, dip them again after drying. The strips may be warmed with a hair dryer or hot plate to dry faster, but this can cause brown spots. Students will cut the strips into 10 pieces, so they only need one 20 cm strip. You can search the internet for "cabbage juice indicator colors" to find the color chart because they cannot be printed in a black-and-white book. Generally, starting from low pH to high, they go red, pink, purple (neutral), green, and yellow.

pH paper made from red cabbage is far superior to litmus paper. It has a whole range of colors that allows students to estimate pH instead of just determining if a solution is an acid or a base. Colors fade over time and disappear completely in several months. Students cannot test hydrogen peroxide or bleach because they turn the paper white.

Post-Lab Questions

1. Answers vary, but most students find one of each.
2. Acids are the most common because they are sour.
3. Rubbing alcohol shows a pH of 7. Most mixtures without water will show a pH of 7. Technically, the pH values of mixtures other than water are not defined. The pH concept is limited to water solutions.

ACTIVITY 48: TITRATION LAB

Objective
Students will titrate a known concentration of baking soda with vinegar to find out the concentration of the vinegar.

Purpose
Students will practice using the formula $M_1V_1 = M_2V_2$ to calculate the molarity of an unknown solution.

Materials
Baking soda, balance (Activity 2), vinegar, syringe

Notes
This should not be the only titration that students do. Titrations are important in college chemistry and students should do several types. I have them do this titration at home. Then they do a titration simulation that I wrote and put on my website (*http://mysite.verizon.net/res6pa7x/titration.swf*; if this URL changes, simply do a search online for "titration.swf"). Then students do a standard acid/base titration with phenolphthalein. Then they do an iodometric titration of vitamin C. Then they do a titration with pH probes and do titration curves and the first derivative of the curve.

Post-Lab Questions
1. The vinegar would be stronger. Whichever one requires the smaller amount is more concentrated. For comparison, if 20 people can beat up 25 people, the 20 people must be stronger.
2. Answers will vary.
3. Vinegar is approximately 5% acetic acid. Five grams (5 g) of acetic acid is 0.08 moles in 0.10 liters, which is 0.80 molar. Sources of error include measuring accurately with the syringe, identifying the exact endpoint, using varying concentrations of different brands of vinegar, and maintaining accuracy when mixing the baking soda solution.

ACTIVITY 49: REDOX REACTION LAB

Objective

Students will allow steel wool to rust overnight and measure approximately how much oxygen is consumed.

Purpose

Students will see that in a rusting reaction (redox), the metal is oxidized and the oxygen is reduced.

Materials

Steel wool, test tube, glass of water

Notes

The atmospheric application of this lab is a valuable one. Most students think air and oxygen are the same. I've heard a lot of SCUBA divers refer to their tanks as oxygen tanks. Students can see that the air is only approximately 20% oxygen.

Many people use candles under a glass and rising water to demonstrate this concept, but that is not a good demonstration. The rising of the water in that version of the demonstration is dominated by the heat of the candle flame, not the burning of the oxygen. This can be demonstrated easily by using one, two, or three candles. If oxygen was the dominant factor, water would rise to the same level in all three candles. It does not. For a longer treatment of this and other science misconceptions, do an internet search for my Science Misconception Podcast. It is presently located at *http://scienceinquirer.wikispaces.com/misconception* (although the URL may have changed by the time you read this).

Topic: Redox Reactions
Go to: *www.scilinks.org*
Code: THC40

Post-Lab Questions

1. Oxygen, O_2
2. $Fe + O_2 \rightarrow Fe_2O_3$
3. Iron was oxidized, oxygen was reduced, iron is the reducing agent, and oxygen is the oxidizing agent.

Atmospheric Chemistry Application

1. Answers will vary, but approximately 20%.
2. A synthesis reaction occurred in which the solid iron reacted with the gaseous oxygen to form iron (III) oxide. The ideal gas law says that if the number of moles of gas is reduced, pressure is reduced. Because there is unequal pressure (higher on the outside than inside), water is forced up the tube. Oxygen makes up approximately 20% of the atmosphere, so it rises approximately 20% of the volume.
3. Answers will vary.

ACTIVITY 50: ADHESION AND COHESION LAB

Objectives

Students will put drops of liquids on different surfaces and see if they bead up or wet the surface.

Topic: Intermolecular Forces
Go to: *www.scilinks.org*
Code: THC41

Purpose

Students will see that the relative strength of adhesive and cohesive forces determines whether or not a liquid will wet a surface. Students will be introduced to intermolecular forces.

Materials

Water, paper towel, plastic wrap, wax paper, glass, cooking oil, straw, syrup

Notes

This is a very good lab to show that chemistry is all around us. Most students have probably noticed this effect before but have never thought about the chemistry of it. Answers may be different because some paper towels are coated on one side and there are many different types of glass with different coatings on them.

Procedure

1. a. Water and paper towel
    b. Water and water
    c. Water and water
    d. Answers may vary, but likely water and water.
2. a. Oil and paper towel
    b. Oil and oil
    c. Oil and oil
    d. Oil and oil
3. Water and straw
4. Syrup and straw (This is a very small effect, so do not penalize students for a wrong answer. It is not as important for them to get the right answer as to follow the correct thought process.)

Post-Lab Questions

1. Forces between fluid and plant are stronger and help draw the liquid up the tubes.
2. Water and water. The water-to-water attraction is stronger; otherwise the insect would get wet and wink. The water-water attraction (surface tension) allows small, light objects to rest on the surface.
3. Water and coffee filter. The water-to-paper attraction is stronger. If the water-water attraction was stronger, the paper would not be able to pull the water up out of the cup.

ACTIVITY 42: CARTESIAN DIVER LAB

QUESTION ❓

Why does the Cartesian diver sink?

SAFETY 🩹

Clean up any spills immediately. Do not consume the mustard or drink the water when finished.

MATERIALS 📏

2 L soda bottle, mustard packet, paper clip, water, syringe

PROCEDURE 🔧

A Cartesian diver is a device made by putting a flexible object in a plastic bottle filled with water so that when the bottle is squeezed, the object sinks to the bottom. In this lab, you will use a mustard packet as the flexible object and a paper clip as the weight. There is some air trapped in the mustard packet that allows it to change shape when the bottle is squeezed.

First, you will find the volume of the mustard packet. Fill a cup with water and let it overflow a little. Put an empty container (such as another cup) under the full cup and put the mustard packet in the full cup. Push the packet down with the tip of a pencil so that it is just below the surface of the water but so the pencil does not go under. Catch the overflowing water and measure it with your syringe. Record the volume in your data chart. Find the mass of the mustard packet and record it in your data chart.

To build your Cartesian diver, fill a soda bottle (volume does not matter) completely with water. Put the mustard packet in the full bottle and let some of the water overflow. Cap the bottle tightly. Gradually start to squeeze the bottle. You probably will not be able to get the mustard packet to sink.

Repeat the entire procedure, but this time with a paper clip attached to the mustard packet. You can get the mustard packet to hover in the middle of the bottle (this is called neutral buoyancy) or sink all the way to the bottom (negative buoyancy).

Data

Volume of mustard packet	_____ ml
Mass of mustard packet	_____ g
Mass of mustard packet with paper clip	_____ g

Post-Lab Questions

1. What is the density of the mustard packet alone?
2. What must the density of the mustard packet be for it to hover in the middle?
3. Does the mass of the mustard packet change as you squeeze the bottle?
4. What must the volume of the packet be for it to have neutral buoyancy?
5. Why did you have to add the paper clip to get the packet to sink?

Extension

If you have a bottle that is oval or rectangular, you can make a Cartesian riser, a diver that sits on the bottom and rises when you squeeze the sides of the bottle. You can use a shampoo, mouthwash, or dishwashing liquid bottle. Put enough paper clips on the mustard packet so that it just barely sinks to the bottom on its own. Then squeeze the short sides of the bottle and it will rise to the top. Can you explain why?

ACTIVITY 43: PRESSURE LAB

QUESTION

How strong is air pressure?

SAFETY

Hold the cup tightly so as not to drop it and break it. Clean up any spills immediately. Perform this activity over a sink or trash can in case the water falls out. Do not drink the water.

MATERIALS

Drinking glass, water, 3 × 5 in. card, ruler

PROCEDURE

In this lab, you will use an index card to hold a column of water in place with the help of air pressure. To do this, you will need a 3 × 5 in. index card and a plastic cup whose mouth the card can cover. You can measure items in inches for this lab because in life you will see pressure measured in pounds per square inch, and you should at least be familiar with those units.

Fill the cup completely with water and put the index card over the top. Holding the index card, flip the cup over (hold it over a sink just in case). Now release the index card and everything should stay right where it is.

Calculations

1. Measure the diameter of the cup that you are using in inches. Normally, we do not use inches in science classes, but we will make an exception in this case.
2. Calculate the area of the mouth of the cup using the formula $A = \pi r^2$.
3. Air pressure is 14.7 lbs/in.^{2}. Use the area of the mouth of the cup from question #2 and the equation *force = (pressure)(area)* to figure out how many pounds of air pressure are pushing up on the card.
4. Assume that you have a half pound of water in the cup. How many pounds per square inch are pushing down on the card due to the water?

Post-Lab Questions

1. Which is pushing harder, the water pushing down or the air pushing up?
2. Why do the water and index card not fall down?
3. How many pounds of water could theoretically be held up with a card that is the size of a sheet of paper (8.5 × 11 in.)?

ACTIVITY 44: BOYLE'S LAW LAB

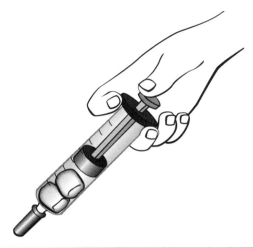

QUESTION ?

How do different items react to changes in pressure?

SAFETY

Do not eat or drink any materials. Wear goggles in case the plunger flies out of the syringe. Clean up spills immediately.

MATERIALS

Syringe, water, marshmallows, soda

PROCEDURE

In this lab, you will investigate how different substances react when compressed or expanded in a syringe. You will put air, water, marshmallows, and soda in the syringe and make observations.

1. Air: Put the cap on the syringe with the plunger at the halfway point, put your finger over the end, or put on a cap (if available) and press down on the plunger.
        Q1: How far were you able to squeeze the air?
    With the tip still covered, pull the syringe out as far as you can.
        Q2: How far were you able to expand the air?

2. Water: Fill the syringe with water, trying not to allow any air bubbles. Put the cap on the syringe, or put your finger over the end and press down on the plunger.

    Q3: How far were you able to squeeze the water?

    Q4: Which is more compressible, gases or liquids?

3. Marshmallow: Put the small marshmallow in the syringe. Put the cap on the syringe or put your finger over the end.

    Q5: What happens to the marshmallow when you pull out the plunger?

    Q6: What happens to the marshmallow when you push down on the plunger?

    Q7: Explain your observations about the marshmallow.

4. Soda: Put some soda in the syringe and put the cap on it (be sure that the soda isn't flat before you begin).

    Q8: What happens to the soda bubbles when you push down on the plunger?

    Q9: What happens to the soda bubbles when you pull the plunger out?

    Q10: Explain your observations about the soda.

ACTIVITY 45: FINGER THERMOMETER

QUESTION ❓

Can your finger be used as an accurate thermometer?

SAFETY ◈

Only warm water and refrigerator-cold water should be used for this activity. If the activity becomes uncomfortable at any time, stop immediately. Clean up any spills to prevent slipping and falling.

MATERIALS ⧉

3 cups with cold water, room temperature water, and warm water

PROCEDURE 👣

You can put your finger in a cup of water and determine if it is hot or cold. But how accurate is your finger as a thermometer? In this activity, you will find out if your finger is more of a temperature detector or a detector of changes in temperature.

1. Get three drinking cups ready with a wide enough mouth that allows you to put your finger in the water.
2. In the left cup, put cold water either from the refrigerator or tap water with a couple of ice cubes in it. In the middle cup, put room-temperature tap water. In the right cup, put warm tap water.
3. Put a finger from your left hand in the left (cold) cup and put your right finger in the right (warm) cup of water. Wait 30 seconds, then put both fingers in the middle cup. Think about how the water feels to each of the fingers.

Post-Lab Questions

1. How did the water feel to your left hand? How did the water feel to your right hand?
2. Is your skin a temperature detector or a change-in-temperature detector?
3. How is this similar to the optical illusions where you stare at a colored object for 30 seconds and then stare at a blank wall? If you have not seen one of these before, use your favorite online search engine to search for "American Flag Optical Illusion."

Extension

Find a smooth object (such as a sheet protector or other smooth piece of plastic) and a sheet of paper. Set the smooth object near carpet. For 30 seconds, rub the fingers of your left hand on the carpet and the fingers of your right hand on the smooth object. After 30 seconds, rub the fingers of both hands on the sheet of paper. How does the paper feel to your left hand? How does it feel to your right hand? How is this similar to the finger thermometer?

ACTIVITY 46: EXPANSION AND CONTRACTION

QUESTION ❓

What happens to the volume of a gas as its temperature changes?

SAFETY 🩹

Be very careful with the hot water. Balloons can be a choking hazard for small children; keep them out of the reach of children, and if they pop, throw away all of the pieces.

MATERIALS 📏

Small balloon, small bucket, water, large container, syringe, tongs or stick

PROCEDURE 👣

In this lab, you will put a balloon in the freezer and see what happens to its volume. If room temperature and the temperature of your freezer were far enough apart, you could use these to values to extrapolate what the Celsius value of absolute zero is, but they are not.

1. Fill a small water balloon about halfway with air. Fill a small bucket, such as a margarine container, all the way to the top with water and place it inside a larger container. Push the balloon under water and collect all of the water that spills over. Measure the water by pouring it into your syringe. Pour several times if necessary.

2. Now put the balloon in the freezer for about an hour and put a bucket of water in the refrigerator.
3. Repeat the measurement process, but using the refrigerated water this time, and measure the spilled water.
4. Now put the balloon in a sink under a stream of hot water from the faucet for a minute or two. Have a bucket of hot water ready for the measurement. Do not put your hands in the hot water; use tongs or a stick to push it down. Repeat the volume-measuring procedure again.

Data

Volume of balloon at room temperature _____ ml

Volume of balloon from freezer _____ ml

Volume of the hot balloon _____ ml

Post-Lab Questions

1. Did the balloon get bigger or smaller in the freezer? By how much?
2. Imagine that room temperature was 22°C and the freezer was −5°C. What would be your estimate for absolute zero (the temperature at which the volume would be zero)? How close is that to the real answer? You may have to draw a graph to measure this.
3. Why was hot water used to measure the hot balloon and cold water used to measure the cold balloon?

ACTIVITY 47: pH PAPER LAB

QUESTION ⁇

What are the pH values of common substances around the house?

SAFETY

Wear goggles if you use any chemicals that are not kitchen ingredients in foods. Do not dip the papers into the substances you are testing to avoid contaminating them. Instead, use a toothpick or similar object to put some of the substance on the paper.

MATERIALS

pH paper made from paper towels and red (purple) cabbage juice

PROCEDURE

In this lab, you will use pH paper made from the juice of a red (purple) cabbage. Because of a chemical called anthocyanin, red cabbage juice acts as a good indicator of acid and base over a wide range of pH values. Blue and green coloring indicates that a solution is basic or alkaline. Red colors indicate that a solution is acidic.

Cut your piece of pH paper into 10 pieces and use it to test 8 chemicals around the house (you have two extras just in case). You may test liquids or solids dissolved in water. You cannot test anything that will bleach the color of the paper (peroxide, bleach, some cleaning products) or something so thick and dark that the paper cannot be seen (ketchup, barbecue sauce, etc.). Do not use any hazardous substances, such as pesticides, pharmaceuticals, poisons, or strong cleaning chemicals. Put one drop of the substance to be tested on the pH paper and immediately record the color. The colors will change with time; record the color immediately after the test.

Data

For each test, you should record the following data:

- Substance tested
- Color that the substance turned the pH paper
- Whether the substance is a strong acid, a weak acid, neutral, a weak base, or a strong base

Post-Lab Questions

1. Did you find at least one of each (acid, neutral, base)?
2. Of things that we eat or drink, which is most common: acid, neutral, or base?
3. Did you find anything other than water that was neutral?

Extension

If it rains any time soon, test the rain water to find out if it is an acid or a base. If there is a body of water near you, measure the pH of the lake, river, or ocean and see if it is related to the pH of the rain.

ACTIVITY 48: TITRATION LAB

QUESTION ❓

What is the concentration of vinegar?

SAFETY 🩹

Goggles are required for this activity. Do not consume any of the chemicals used in this lab. Clean up any spills, and wash your hands when finished.

MATERIALS 📏

Baking soda, balance (Activity 2), vinegar, syringe

PROCEDURE 👣

A titration is a laboratory technique in which a known concentration of one chemical is used to figure out the concentration of another chemical. An acid and a base are usually used in a titration, but others are used as well. For example, vitamin C can be titrated with iodine until the color changes. A solution that conducts electricity can be titrated until it no longer conducts. Normally, when titrating an acid and a base, an acid-base indicator is used, which changes colors when the equilibrium point is reached (the equilibrium point is when all of one chemical has been used up in reacting with the other chemical). In this lab, you will use vinegar (acetic acid, $HC_2H_3O_2$) and baking soda ($NaHCO_3$). The good thing about the reaction between these two is that it produces bubbles of carbon dioxide when they react. As a result, you do not really need an indicator to tell you when the reaction is complete; you can watch for the bubbles to stop forming. In this lab, you will calculate the approximate concentration of the vinegar from the measured concentration of the baking soda.

Molarity is how we measure in chemistry the concentration of a solution. Molarity is calculated by dividing the number of moles of the solute by the number of liters of the solvent.

1.   Measure 3.0 g of baking soda by putting 3.0 ml of water on one side of the balance and adding baking soda until it balances.
2.   Add 25 ml of water to the baking soda and pour it into another cup. Fill the syringe with vinegar.
3.   Slowly add the vinegar drop by drop and watch for bubbles to form. When you think they have stopped, record the volume of vinegar delivered, but continue adding vinegar just in case you were wrong.
4.   Once the bubbles have definitely stopped, write down what volume of vinegar you used.

Calculations

1.   Calculate the molar mass of baking soda. Molar mass = _____
2.   Calculate how many moles of baking soda were used. Moles of baking soda used = _____
3.   According to the balanced equation for this reaction,
     $$HC_2H_3O_2 + NaHCO_3 \rightarrow H_2O + CO_2 + NaC_2H_3O_2,$$
     one mole of vinegar reacts with one mole of baking soda. Knowing that the number of moles of vinegar is equal to the number of moles of baking soda, calculate the molarity of the vinegar.

     Moles of vinegar = _____ moles
     Volume of vinegar = _____ ml
     Molarity of vinegar = _____ M

Post-Lab Questions

1.   If this lab required 20 ml of vinegar for 25 ml of baking soda, which solution would be more concentrated? Explain.
2.   Which solution was more concentrated? Explain.
3.   Your teacher will give you the generally accepted concentration for vinegar. What was your percent error? What were some sources of that error?

ACTIVITY 49: REDOX REACTION LAB

QUESTION ❓

What percentage of air is composed of oxygen?

SAFETY

Clean up any broken glass immediately. Keep steel wool away from sparks and flames; it is flammable.

MATERIALS

Steel wool, test tube, glass of water

PROCEDURE

Redox is short for reduction/oxidation reaction. A redox reaction is one in which the oxidation state of atoms changes during the reaction. For example, when $H_2 + O_2 \rightarrow H_2O$, the reactants each have an oxidation state of 0. On the product side, the hydrogen has an oxidation state of +1 and the oxygen has an oxidation state of –2. The reactant whose oxidation state increased (hydrogen in this case) is said to have been oxidized and is called the reducing agent. The reactant whose oxidation state decreased (oxygen in this case) is said to have been reduced and is called the oxidizing agent.

1. Wad up a ball of steel wool the size of a small marble, wet it, and stuff it inside a test tube.
2. Invert the test tube in the glass of water and leave it overnight.
3. The following morning, make observations about what happened. Measure how high the water level rose. Make observations about the changes in the steel wool as well.

Post-Lab Questions

1. What was the substance that reacted with the steel wool? (Hint: It was not water.) Write the formula for the substance.
2. A reaction went on in the test tube. Write and balance the formula for that chemical reaction. Assume that steel wool is mostly iron (III) or Fe^{+3}.
3. In that reaction, what was oxidized? What was reduced? What was the oxidizing agent? What was the reducing agent?

Atomspheric Chemistry Application

1. Compare the height of the water to the height of the test tube. What percentage of the height of the test tube did the water rise?
2. What caused that rise in water level? Try to use as many of the following terms in your explanation: *gas*, *solid*, *pressure*, *ideal gas law*, *unequal*, *synthesis*, and *moles*.
3. The percentage rise in water is proportional to the percentage of oxygen in the air. Find in a book or online what percentage of the air is oxygen and compare this figure to your percentage in #1.

ACTIVITY 50: ADHESION AND COHESION LAB

QUESTION ❓

Why do some liquids form a bead?

SAFETY

Clean up any spills or broken glass immediately to prevent slips and falls. Do not contaminate the bottle of oil by placing droppers in it. Pour some into another container first, and do not pour the excess back in the bottle. Do not eat or drink any of the materials from this activity.

MATERIALS

Water, paper towel, plastic wrap, wax paper, glass, cooking oil, straw, syrup

PROCEDURE

Due to intermolecular forces, molecules are attracted to each other. Some molecules are strongly attracted to molecules of their own kind (cohesion). Some molecules are more strongly attracted to other molecules (adhesion). To remember the difference, just recall that adhesives are things such as tape and glue that stick to other objects.

Several phenomena can be explained by these forces. The way that water "beads up" after your car is waxed is one example. Surface tension and the meniscus in a thin cylinder of water are other examples.

You have probably noticed that sometimes when you put a drop of water on an object, it can either spread out, soak in, or wet the object, or it can stay as a droplet with distinct edges. When water wets an object, the adhesive forces are stronger than the cohesive forces (the liquid is attracted to the object more than it is attracted to itself). When water forms droplets, the cohesive forces are stronger than the adhesive forces. When a liquid forms a meniscus that curves downward (concave) toward the center, the cohesive forces are stronger than the adhesive forces. When the liquid forms a meniscus that gets higher in the middle (convex), the cohesive forces are stronger than the adhesive forces.

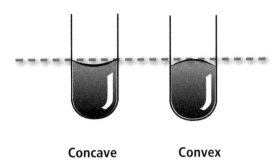

Concave   **Convex**

1. Put a droplet of water on each of the following items, and note whether it wets the items or forms a droplet.

    a. Paper towel
        Which is stronger, the attractive force between water and water or between water and a paper towel?
    b. Plastic wrap
        Which is stronger, the attractive force between water and water, or between water and plastic wrap?
    c. Wax paper
        Which is stronger, the attractive force between water and water, or between water and wax paper?
    d. Glass
        Which is stronger, the attractive force between water and water, or between water and glass?

2. Repeat each of the above tests with a drop of cooking oil.

    a. Which is stronger, the attractive force between oil and oil, or between oil and the paper towel?
    b. Which is stronger, the attractive force between oil and oil, or between oil and plastic wrap?
    c. Which is stronger, the attractive force between oil and oil, or between oil and wax paper?
    d. Which is stronger, the attractive force between oil and oil, or between oil and glass?

3. Place the end of a transparent straw in water, put your thumb over the end, and draw the meniscus that you see (look closely). Which is stronger, the forces between water and water, or between water and the straw?
4. Place the end of a transparent straw in thick syrup (such as Karo syrup), put your thumb over the end, and draw the meniscus that you see (look closely). Which is stronger, the forces between syrup and syrup, or between syrup and the straw?
5. Dispose of small amounts of leftover cooking oil in the trash.

Post-Lab Questions

1. Part of the explanation for how nutrients get from the roots of a plant out to its extremities lies in intermolecular forces. Would you say that the forces between fluid and fluid are stronger than the forces between fluid and plant, or vice versa? Explain.
2. Some small bugs can walk on the surface of the water without breaking through. Which is stronger, the force between water and water, or between water and bug? Explain.
3. Earlier, you did a paper chromatography lab in which water climbed up a coffee filter. Which is stronger, the attraction between water and water, or between water and coffee filter? Explain.

MATERIALS LIST FOR STUDENTS

Anything with a ❏ next to it will be returned at the end of the year. Everything else will be used up throughout the year. You will be charged for any of the returnable items not returned at the end of the year, just like you would for a textbook.

- ❏ Goggles
- ❏ Several zip-top bags
- ❏ Plastic centimeter ruler
- ❏ Small plastic cups (to-go salsa containers)
- ❏ 50–60 cc syringe
- ❏ Syringe cap
- Thread (approximately 2 meters)
- ❏ Washers (either 6 small or 3 large)
- ❏ Rubber ball
- Sugar packet
- Salt packet (2 if small)
- Bag of salt, sand, Styrofoam, and iron (see p. 45)
- ❏ 6 marbles
- 4 coffee filters
- Transparent drinking straw
- 2 Wint-O-Green Life Savers
- 2 Alka-Seltzer or other effervescent tablets
- Cornstarch (approximately 6 spoonfuls)
- Epsom salt (approximately 3 spoonfuls)
- ❏ 2 mechanical pencil leads (0.7 mm)
- ❏ 9 V battery (keep in a zip-top bag to avoid shorting)
- ❏ 9 V battery clip or 2 wires (1 red and 1 black)
- Baking soda (approximately 6 spoonfuls, for multiple activities)
- 2 anodized nails
- 2 uncoated iron nails (called bright nails at Home Depot)
- Small wad of steel wool (must be real steel wool, not copper or rust-proof wool)
- ❏ Mustard packet
- ❏ Paper clip (small)
- 3 × 5 in. card
- 2 or 3 small marshmallows (to be handed out just before the activity)
- Red cabbage pH paper (See p. 203 for instructions. This can take a couple of days to make and dry, and it should be handed out shortly before the activity.)

Materials Provided by Student

(Let your teacher know if you do not have one of these items, and they will make arrangements to get you what is needed.)

- Various coins
- Timer (stopwatch, cell phone, secondhand on watch or clock)
- Stack of paper
- Pen or pencil
- Scissors
- Dishwashing liquid
- Cooking oil
- Drinking glass
- Sugar
- Food coloring or other colored liquid
- Bowl
- Uncooked rice, popcorn kernels, or dry beans
- Compact disk
- Shoe box
- Sugar
- Salt
- Oil
- Rubbing alcohol
- Paper towel
- Household ammonia
- Vinegar

DUPLICATION PAGES

Students will need to either cut out or write on the following sheets. Students should be given extra copies of these pages so they do not tear pages out of the lab manual or write in the manual.

Activity 11

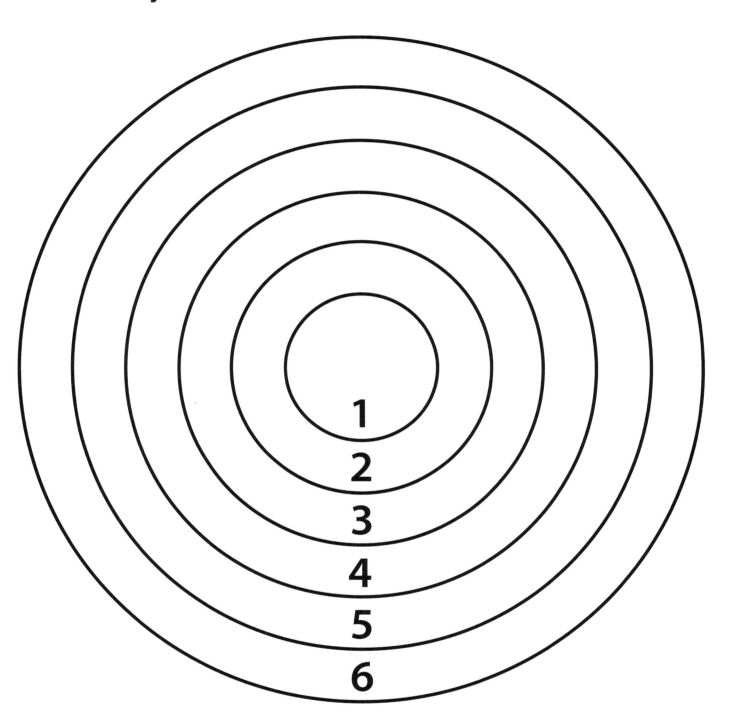

Activity 12

α	α	α	α	α	α	α	α	α	α
α	α	α	α	α	α	α	α	α	α
α	α	α	α	α	α	α	α	α	α
α	α	α	α	α	α	α	α	α	α
α	α	α	α	α	α	α	α	α	α
α	α	α	α	α	α	α	α	α	α
α	α	α	α	α	α	α	α	α	α
α	α	α	α	α	α	α	α	α	α
α	α	α	α	α	α	α	α	α	α
α	α	α	α	α	α	α	α	α	α

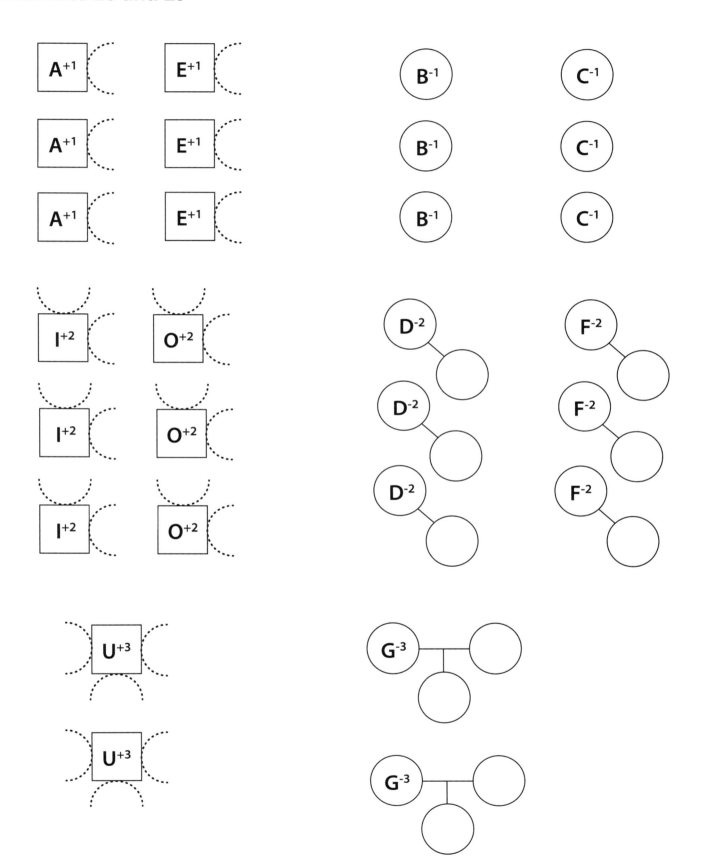

INDEX

Note: Page numbers in *italic type* refer to figures or tables.